I0605282

First published in the UK 2024 by Sona Books an imprint of Danann Media Publishing Ltd.

Proof reader: Juliette O'Neill

Image credits:

P28-31: Angela Spain
P34-37: Janathan Stewart
43: Simon owen
P46-47: Angela Spain
P56-61: Barry Marsden
P62-65: Janathan Stewart
P66-73: Angela Spain
P74-81: Sussie Bell
P88-93: Jonathan Stewart
P100: Claire Lloyd Davies
P102-103: futurecontenthub.com.
P108-198: ti-mediacontent.com
P110-113: Angela Spain
P116-121: Ayne Jackson

CAT NO: **SON0623**
ISBN: **978-1-915343-97-0**

Made in EU.

Create your own

CROCHET BLANKETS

The Tale of Tom Kitten
The Tailor of Gloucester
The Tale of Peter Rabbit
The Tale of Ginger and Pickles

Welcome to

Create your own CROCHET BLANKETS

Have you always wanted to crochet your own blankets, but didn't know where to begin?

In *Create your own Crochet Blankets*, we take you through everything you need to know to complete your crafty project! Whether you want to crochet a blanket for yourself or as a gift for a loved one, you will find a variety of patterns inside to make lovely, handmade blankets suitable for all ages and occasions.

Contents

Discover a range of versatile and colourful crochet blankets suitable for all skill levels

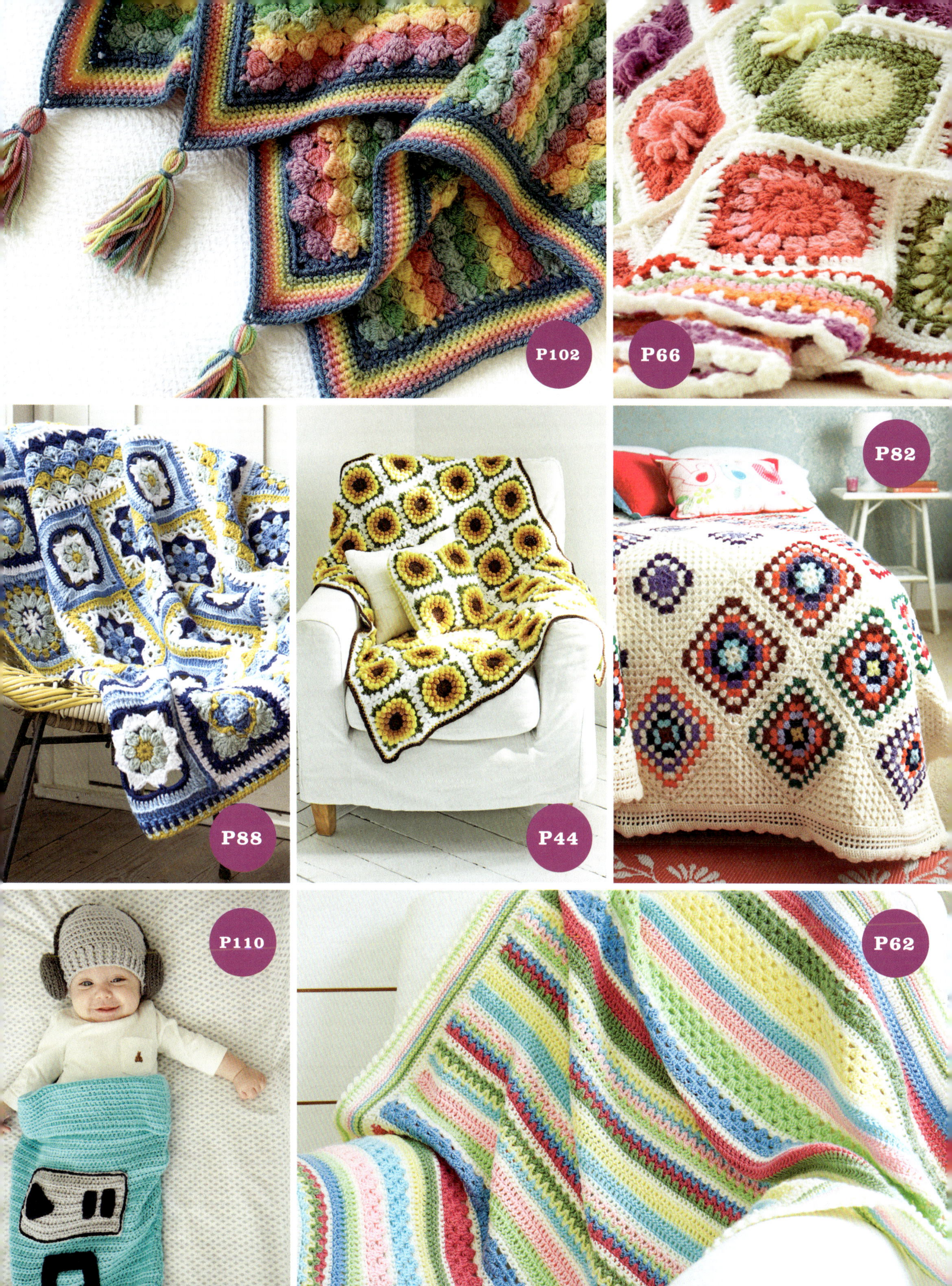

P102
P66
P82
P88
P44
P110
P62

Getting started

Everything you need to know to get started in crochet, from tools to stitches.

The essentials

Learn the basics to get you started on your crocheting journey

Holding your hook

OVERHAND (KNIFE GRIP)

This technique is also known as the knife grip, as you grip the crochet hook as if you're holding a knife. Place your hand over the hook, then support the handle in your chosen palm.

UNDERHAND (PENCIL GRIP)

For this technique, hold the hook like a pencil (hence the name pencil grip). Hold the thumb rest between your thumb and index finger and then let the handle rest on top of your hand.

Holding your yarn

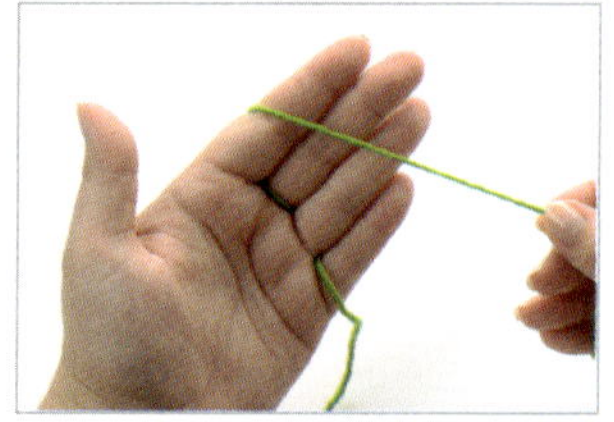

THE LOOSE-YARN HOLD

Holding the end of the yarn in your right hand and with your left palm facing you, weave the yarn in front of your little finger, behind your ring finger, in front of your middle finger and behind your index finger.

THE PINKY HOLD

Looping the yarn once around your little finger may help you to keep a secure grip. Follow the instructions for the loose-yarn hold, but begin by looping the yarn around your little finger clockwise.

Make a slipknot

MAKE A LOOP

Wrap the yarn once around two of your fingers on your left hand to form a loop, making sure to leave a tail of at least 10cm (or longer if your pattern calls for it).

DRAW UP A LOOP

Take the loop off the hook and grip between your thumb and fingers. Insert your hook from right to left, catch the working yarn and pull through to make a loop on your hook.

PULL TO CLOSE THE LOOP

Grip the tail and the working yarn and pull them tight to form a knot. Pull the working yarn to tighten the loop around your hook. It needs to be able to move up and down your hook so don't pull too tight.

Chain stitch (ch)

YARN OVER & DRAW UP LOOP

Starting with a slipknot, move your hook underneath your yarn and pull this through the loop already on your hook.

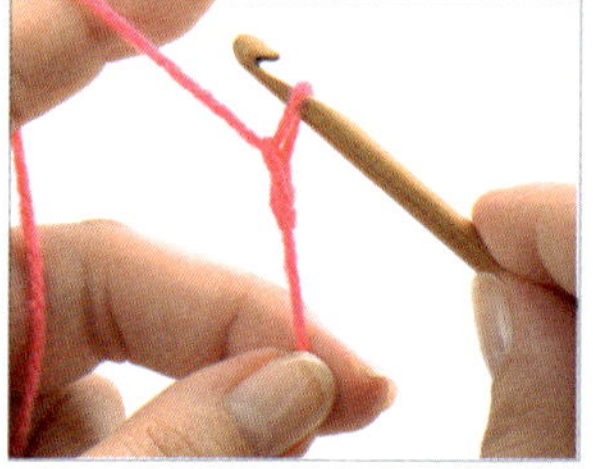

KEEP GOING

Keep going to create a chain of the length needed in your pattern. Try not to make the stitches too tight as this will make it difficult when working subsequent rows. Keep the stitches even or you will get an uneven edge on your piece.

Counting chains

To count the chains, identify the Vs on the side that's facing you. Each of these is one chain. The V above the slipknot is your first chain, but don't count the loop on your hook. This is the working loop and does not count as a chain. If you are creating a very long chain , it might help to mark every 10 or 20 stitches with a stitch marker.

Slip stich (ss/sl/st)

INTO CHAIN
Insert your hook into the second chain from the hook. Yarn over (yo). Pull your hook back through the chain. There should be two loops on your hook.

PULL THROUGH Avoiding the urge to yarn over, continue to pull the yarn through the second loop on the hook. You have completed the stitch and should have one loop on your hook.

Left handed?

All the tutorials in this book can be followed by left-handed crocheters. Simply reverse the instructions and hold the picture tutorials up to a mirror to see how you should be working. So every time you see 'Right' replace it with 'Left' and every time you see 'Clockwise' replace with 'Counterclockwise' (and vice versa)

Working the foundation chain

FRONT OF THE CHAIN
Looking at the front side of your chain, you will see a row of sideways Vs, each with two loops - a top loop and a bottom loop.

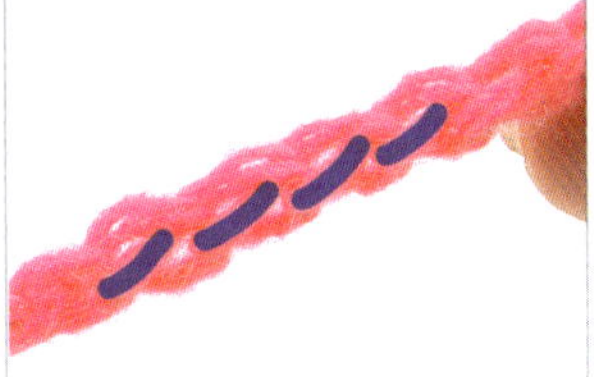

BACK OF THE CHAIN
When you look at the back side of the chain, you will see a line of bumps in between the loops. These are called the back bumps.

It doesn't matter which method you use as long as you are consistent when moving along the chain. Working under the top loop is the easiest method for beginners, but does not create as neat an edge as working under the back bumps.

Method 1: TOP LOOP
For this method, hook under the top loop only.

Method 2: TOP TWO LOOPS
Hooking under both the top loop and the back bump is sometimes referred to as the top two loops of the chain

Method 3: TOP LOOP AND BACK BUMP
Turn over your chain so that the back bumps are facing you. Insert your hook under the back bump.

UK and US terms

Confusingly, patterns can follow either UK or US naming conventions. To make things even more difficult, the same name is used to mean different stitches under either convention.

Most patterns will state whether they are using US or UK terminology, but if not, checking the pattern's country of origin may be a good place to start.

A handy trick to remember is that there is no stitch called a single crochet (sc) in UK terminology, so if you see this on the pattern, then you know it is using US naming conventions.

UK	US
Chain (ch)	Chain (ch)
Double crochet (dc)	Single crochet (sc)
Treble crochet (tr)	Double crochet (dc)
Half treble crochet (htr)	Half double crochet (hdc)
Double treble crochet (dtr)	Triple (treble) crochet (tr)
Slip stitch (sl st/ss)	Slip stitch (sl st/ss)

Double crochet (dc)

INSERT HOOK Working into your foundation chain, find the second chain from your hook and insert your hook.

DRAW UP A LOOP
Yarn over (yo), then draw up a loop. You will now have two loops on your crochet hook.

PULL TO CLOSE THE LOOP
Yarn over and then draw the yarn through both loops on the hook so you have one loop left on your hook. You have now completed the stitch.

Treble crochet (tr)

INSERT HOOK Working into your foundation chain, identify the fourth chain from your hook. Make a yarn over (yo) and then insert your hook into the fourth chain from the hook.

YARN OVER AND DRAW UP A LOOP
Yarn over, then draw up a loop. There should now be three loops on your hook.

YARN OVER AND DRAW UP A LOOP
Yarn over, then draw the yarn through two of the loops on your hook. There should now be two loops on your hook.

COMPLETE THE STITCH
Yarn over and then draw the yarn through the two loops left on the hook. You have completed the stitch and should have one loop on your hook.

Double treble crochet (dtr)

MAKE A LOOP
Working into your foundation chain, identify the fifth chain from your hook. Yarn over twice and insert your hook into the fifth chain from the hook. Yarn over and draw up a loop. There should be four loops on your hook. Yarn over, then draw the yarn through two of the loops on your hook. There should now be three loops on your hook.

DRAW UP A LOOP
Yarn over, then draw the yarn through two of the loops on your hook again. There should now be two loops on your hook. Yarn over, then draw the yarn through the two loops on your hook. There should now be one loop on your hook. You have completed the stitch.

Half treble crochet (htr)

INSERT HOOK
Working into your foundation chain, identify the third chain from your hook. Make a yarn over (yo) and then insert your hook into the third chain from the hook.

YARN OVER AND DRAW UP A LOOP
Yarn over, then draw up a loop. There should now be three loops on your hook. Yarn over, then draw the yarn through all three loops on your hook. The stitch is now complete and there should be one loop on your hook.

Identifying stitches

There are two ways to count stitches: either by counting the Vs along the top of the work or by counting the posts. If you count the Vs, make sure you never count the loop that is on your hook. When counting either Vs or posts, you must take careful consideration when you come to the turning chain. If it is counted as a stitch in your pattern, then count it, but if not, leave it out.

Working rows

UNDER BOTH
Hooking under the front and back loops of the stitch is the most common way to work into a row. Use this method unless told otherwise.

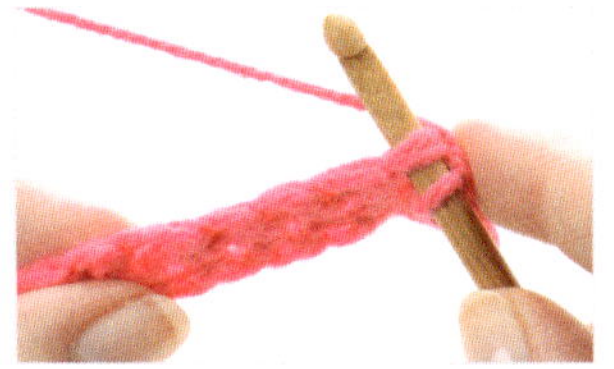

INSERT YOUR HOOK
After the turning chain, insert your hook so that it goes in under both the front and back loops of the V.

FRONT AND BACK LOOPS ONLY (FLO AND BLO)
Sometimes a pattern will say to work into Front or Back loops only. Doing so will create ridges in your work, for example, you may use FLO/BLO to add ribbing to a hat. To work into Front loops only (FLO) identify the loop closest to you and work into the stitch as normal. For Back loops, use the loop farthest away from you.

Join a new yarn

THE LAST STITCH
When you think you don't have enough yarn left in your current ball, or you need to change colour, begin the last stitch of your current row with the old yarn, but stop before you reach the final step (yo and draw through all loops on hook).

DRAW UP A LOOP
Make a yarn over (yo) with the new ball of yarn and complete the stitch. Leave a tail of at least a 15cm (5.9in) on the new yarn. Continue crocheting with the new yarn, and drop the old yarn. You can hide the ends in the inside of your project.

Changing colour

ALONG THE EDGE
When you're creating stripes by changing colour at the beginning of every row or so, you can leave the unworked yarn dangling at the edge. This way you can pick it up again when you need to. To do this, carry it loosely up the edge of the work in order to begin your new row. Adding an edge or border will hide the carried yarn strands.

OVER THE TOP OF THE OLD YARN If you need to change colours regularly and mid-row, crocheting over the top of the yarn you're not currently using is a good way to keep it concealed and eliminates ends that would need weaving in. This technique is great when you are creating a reversible fabric, as it keeps both sides looking neat.

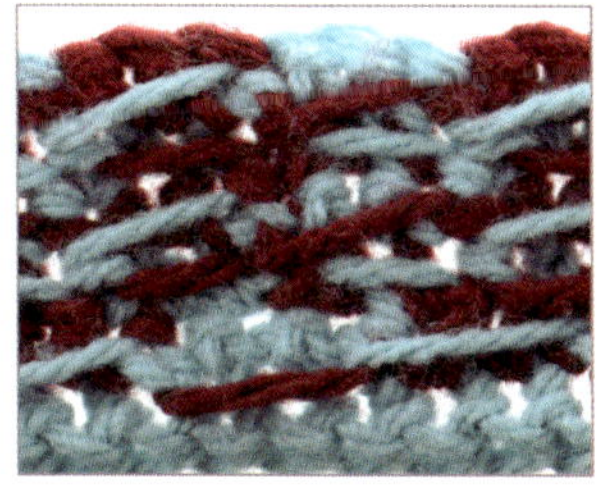

FLOATING STRANDS
If only one side of your final product will be seen, then you can carry the unused colours along the back of the work.Just drop the yarn you're not using, then pick it up again when you need it, loosely bringing it across the back of the work. This works best if the strands are only a few stitches long. If they are longer, cut the threads and weave in instead.

CUTTING THE YARN
If you are putting in a big block of one colour, it's best to cut the yarn and treat it like you're joining a new yarn, then weave in the ends of the yarn at a later stage.

Turning chains

Whenever you turn your work, you will need to create a turning chain to start your next row. When using anything but double crochet, the turning chain always counts as the first stitch (unless specified otherwise), and the next stitch should be created in the second stitch from the hook. Different stitches need different heights of turning chains, to match the height of the stitch about to be made.

Stitch (UK)	Number of turning chains (t-ch)
Double crochet (dc)	1
Half-treble crochet (htr)	2
Treble crochet (tr)	3
Double treble crochet (dtr)	4

Increase

INCREASING IN THE MIDDLE OF A ROW (TREBLES AS EXAMPLE)

Make a treble crochet in the next stitch. Make another treble crochet in the same stitch. You have increased your stitch count by one.

INCREASING AT THE START OF A ROW

As the turning chain normally counts as a stitch (except in dc), increasing at the start of a row is different. To increase, insert your hook into the first stitch at the base of the chain and make the stitch. The stitch you've just made and the turning chain count as two stitches, and you have made an increase.

Decrease

DOUBLE CROCHET TWO STITCHES TOGETHER (DC2TOG)

Insert your hook into the next stitch, as if to make a double crochet. Draw up a loop. Without completing the stitch, insert your hook into the next stitch as if to make another double crochet. Draw up a loop. You should now have three loops on your hook. Yarn over (yo) and draw the loop through all three stitches on your hook. Having worked into two stitches, but only created one, you have decreased by one.

TREBLE CROCHET THREE STITCHES TOGETHER (TR3TOG)

Yarn over and insert your hook into the next stitch, as if to make a treble crochet. Draw up a loop, yarn over and draw through two loops on the hook. There should now be two loops on your hook. *Without completing the stitch, yarn over and insert your hook into the next stitch. Draw up a loop, yarn over and draw through two loops on the hook.* There should now be three loops on your hook. Repeat * to * into the next stitch. There should now be four loops on your hook, yarn over and draw the yarn through all four loops to complete the decrease.

Starting in the round

Method 1: SINGLE CHAIN START

Chain two. Now make a double crochet (dc) into the second chain from your hook. Make the rest of your doubles into the same chain stitch as your first double crochet.

Method 2: MULTIPLE CHAIN START

Make a short chain, depending on the pattern that you're following. Here we have shown five chains. Create a slip stitch (sl st) into the first chain that you created. Work your first round into the middle of the ring you have just made. Now either continue to work in a spiral or connect the last double crochet to the first with a slip stitch, create your turning chains and continue.

Method 3: MAGIC RING (MR)

Also called a magic circle (mc). To begin, create a loop (as if to create a slipknot), hold the yarn where the loop crosses over, with the starting tail in front, and insert your hook from front to back.

- Yarn over with the working yarn and pull up a loop back through to the front. Yarn over your hook again, this time from above the loop, and pull through to create a chain on your ring.
- To create your first dc, insert your hook into the ring, with both the loop and starting tail above your hook. Your stitches will now be created around both yarns. Yarn over and draw up a loop back to the front of the ring. Create your stitch as you would usually. Carry on until you have the number of stitches you need.
- Once you have created all of your stitches, keep your hook in the loop and hold it and your round in your dominant hand. Pull on the starting tail to close the gap.

Working in the round

CONTINUOUS SPIRAL To start each new round, work the first stitch into the top of the first stitch of the last round. Now add your stitch marker into this stitch by slipping it through the loops. Now continue to stitch the rest of your round as stated in the pattern until you reach the stitch before the marker. This is the last stitch of the round.

To start your next round, remove the marker, crochet the stitch as normal and then replace the marker into the stitch you have just created.

When finishing your spiral you will need to smooth out the jump in stitches between rows. To do so, slip stitch into the next stitch. For taller stitches, gradually crochet shorter stitches i.e if you have used tr stitches you will end with a htr, dc, ss.

JOINED ROUNDS

Alternatively you can add a ss at the end of each row which gives the appearance of concentric circles rather than a spiral. If you do this, to create your next round, create a chain to the height of your stitch. One for double, two for half treble, three for treble and so on.

Turned

Not turned

Turn your work

When you create your next rows you have the choice of turning your work or continuing on around the circle (the same as a spiral stitch). Alternatively, you can turn your work at the end of each round, and it will create a slightly different look. After turning your work, you will continue to work each of the rounds the same way.

Fastening off

SECURE YOUR WORK

When you've finished your project, cut the working yarn about 15cm (6in) from the last stitch (or longer if your pattern states). Yarn over (yo) with the tail. Pull the yarn through the loop on your hook, and keep pulling until the cut end goes through the loop. Grab the tail and pull it tight, to close the last loop.
Your stitches are now secure.

Fixing mistakes

UNDO YOUR WORK

When you notice that things have gone awry, take your hook out of the working loop and grab hold of the working yarn. Pull on the working yarn to unravel the stitches one by one. This process is also known as frogging. Keep pulling the working yarn until you've unravelled the mistake, then simply insert your hook into the working loop and begin redoing the work you've just undone, but this time without the mistake!

Joining

Method 1: WHIP STITCH

Hold two pieces together with the wrong sides facing each other. Pass your needle through the V stitches on both pieces from front to back and pull the yarn through. Draw your needle back to the front and repeat. Using a whip stitch will leave a visible line on both sides of the piece. This won't be quite as obvious when you are using the same colour.

Method 2: MATTRESS STITCH

Lay your pieces side-by-side with the right sides facing you. Leaving a 15cm tail, insert your needle into the first edge stitch of the first piece and then down through the edge of the second. Insert your needle down through the first stitch of piece one and up through to the second stitch. Now repeat on piece two. Keep going and a loose 'ladder' will start to form. When you have done about 2.5cm, pull gently on the yarn to draw the two sides together. Repeat until you have reached the end, the seam will be almost invisible.

Method 3: SLIP STITCH OR DOUBLE CROCHET

Insert your hook through the first stitch on both pieces. Complete a slip stitch (or double crochet) and repeat, ensuring you match up the stitches as you go.

- A slip stitch seam is strong, and will be almost invisible from the other side of the work. Slip stitches do not allow for any give, so making them too tight will pucker the fabric.
- Using a double crochet will give a more pronounced edge, giving a more decorative seam. It is also stretchier than a slip stitch join.

Method 4: FLAT SLIP-STITCHED SEAM

Insert your hook from top to bottom through the back loop only on the right-hand piece of fabric. Do the same on your left piece, then yarn over (yo) and pull through both loops on the hook. Repeat until you reach the end. This seam produces a flat row of chain-looking stitches. It's a neat finish and adds a nice little detail to your seams.

To join amigurumi it is helpful to pin your pieces in place. Join using one of the methods above, inserting your needle from bottom to top of the piece you are attaching. Pull tight on the yarn for a seamless join.

Yarn weights

Yarn weight	Properties	Ideal for...
Lace, 2-ply, fingering	Extremely light, Lace yarn produces a very delicate texture on a 2mm (US 0) hook. Bigger hooks will produce a more open fabric.	Lace
Superfine, 3-ply, fingering, baby	Using a very slim hook, Superfine yarn is perfect for lightweight, intricate lace work.	Finely woven socks, shawls, babywear
Fine, 4-ply, sport, baby	Fine yarn is great for socks, and can also be used in items that feature slightly more delicate textures.	Light jumpers, babywear, socks, accessories
Double knit (DK), light worsted, 5/6-ply	An extremely versatile weight yarn, DK can be used to create a wide variety of items and crochets up relatively quickly.	Jumpers, light-weight scarves, blankets, toys
Aran, medium worsted, Afghan, 12-ply	With many yarns in this thickness using a variety of fibres to make them machine washable, Aran yarn is good for garments with thick cabled detail and functional items.	Jumpers, cabled garments, blankets, hats, scarves, mittens
Chunky, bulky, craft, rug, 14-ply	Quick to crochet, chunky yarn is perfect for warm outerwear. Often made from lightweight fibres to prevent drooping.	Rugs, jackets, blankets, hats, legwarmers, winter accessories
Super chunky, super bulky, bulky, roving, 16-ply and upwards	Commonly used with very large hooks, Super chunky yarn crochets up very quickly. Large stitches make mistakes easy to spot.	Heavy blankets, rugs, thick scarves

Hook size conversion table

UK Size	US Size
2mm, 2.25mm	B/1
2.5mm, 2.75mm	C/2
3mm, 3.25mm	D/3
3.5mm	E/4
3.75mm, 4mm	F/5
4mm, 4.25mm	G/6
4.5mm	G/7
5mm	H/8
5.5mm	I/9
6mm	J/10
6.5mm, 7mm	K/10.5
8mm	L/11
9mm	M/13
10mm	N,P/15

Which hook?

Every ball of yarn comes with a recommended hook size, which is printed on the label. Use bigger hooks than this to make a more open stitch, and smaller ones to make a tighter, more compact fabric. We suggest using a smaller hook than recommended for amigurumi projects.

Tension

Tension or gauge is the measure of how many stitches and rows you need to create a specific length and width of crocheted fabric. The size of your hook, weight of your yarn and your own tension while crocheting will all have an effect on any piece that you're creating. If you naturally crochet very tight or loose stitches, then the final product dimensions will be different to those provided in a pattern. Tension square patterns will sometimes be given with your pattern and allow you to work out how tight to make your stitches before you start. Usually these will be 10cm square.

When making things like children's toys or blankets, there is a bit more freedom when following a pattern. However, when creating garments to exact fitted measurements, tension squares are incredibly important.

With amigurumi a loose tension will show the stuffing between the stitches. It's difficult to be too tight with amigurumi, however you should still be able to work stitches reasonably easily. If needed, switch to a smaller hook for a neater finish.

Amigurumi Tension too loose

Amigurumi correct tension

Blocking

Blocking is a process you will use after making many of your flat projects. It sets the stitches in place, adds definition to lace pieces and strengthens any straight edges in your work.

PIN YOUR WORK

No matter which method you choose to use, you will need to pin the corners to the correct measurement for your final piece.

Next pin half way along the edge, and keep doing this until you are happy that the edges are all straight and even. If you are blocking any crocheted segments that are due to be joined, make sure you measure them out so they match when you come to sew them together.

For more refined edging, thread a blocking wire through each of the stitches or row ends along the straight edge of your project.

Method 1: SPRAY BLOCKING

Spray blocking is the easiest and quickest way of blocking your work. Pin and then take a spray bottle and give a few sprays of water until the surface of your work is evenly saturated. Gently pat the surface to help the water absorb into the yarn fibres. Leave your work to dry; this can sometimes take over 24 hours.

Method 2: STEAM BLOCKING

This method requires an iron or handheld steamer. Do not touch the iron to the yarn at any point. Man-made fibres will melt, and all your work and your iron will be damaged. Pin your work then hold an iron about 2.5cm (1in) from the surface of your project. Steam until the entire surface area is moist to the touch. Once done, pat the surface gently with your hands and leave to dry.

Method 3: WET BLOCKING (BEST FOR LACE WORK)

Fill your sink or bath with lukewarm water. You can add in no-rinse wool wash if you wish. Immerse your project in the water, until saturated. Leave it for 20 minutes then take your project out and gently squeeze out the excess liquid. Do not wring your project, as this will stretch it out of shape. Continue until you can remove no more water. Lay a towel on a flat surface and lie your garment flat. Gently roll up your towel to press out even more water. Pin your project to your blocking surface (a foam mat or mattress is ideal) and leave to dry. If working on a straight-edged lace garment you will need to use a lot of pins and/or blocking wire along the edge of to obtain a professional result. The edge will bow if you don't use enough pins and spoil the finish.

Additional useful terms

ASTERISK* /BRACKETS( )
A symbol used to mark a point in a pattern row, usually at the beginning of a set of repeated instructions.

CHART/STITCH DIAGRAM
A visual depiction of a crochet pattern that uses symbols to represent stitches.

CROSSED STITCHES
Two or more tall stitches that are crossed, one in front of the other, to create an X shape.

FIBERFILL
Toy stuffing used to stuff amigurumi projects.

LINKED STITCH
A variation of any standard tall stitch that links the stitch to its neighbour partway up the post to eliminate the gaps between stitches and form a solid fabric.

POST
The vertical stem of a stitch.

POST STITCH
A stitch formed by crocheting around the post of the stitch in the row or round below, so the stitch sits in front of (or behind) the surface of the fabric.

RIGHT SIDE (RS)
The side of a crocheted piece that's visible when finished.

ROUND (RND)
A line of stitches worked around a circular crocheted piece.

ROW
A line of stitches worked across a flat crocheted piece.

SPACE (SP)
A gap formed between or beneath stitches, often seen in lace patterns.

STITCH MARKER
A small tool you can slide into a crochet stitch to mark a position. You can use a scrap of yarn or a hairgrip instead.

TAIL
A short length of unworked yarn left at the start or end of a piece.

V
The two loops at the top of each stitch that form a sideways V shape; standard crochet stitches are worked into both these loops.

WEAVE IN
A method used to secure and hide the yarn tails by stitching them through your crocheted stitches.

WORKING LOOP
The single loop that remains on your hook after completing a crochet stitch.

WRONG SIDE (WS)
The side of a crocheted piece that will be hidden; the inside or back.

YARN WEIGHT
The thickness of the yarn (not the weight of a ball of yarn).

Abbreviations and symbols

UK stitch name	Abbreviation	Symbol	Description
back loop	BL		The loop furthest from you at the top of the stitch.
back post double crochet	BPdc		Yarn over, insert the hook from the back to the front, then to the back around the post of the next stitch, yarn over and draw up a loop, (yarn over and draw through two loops) twice.
chain(s)	ch(s)		Yarn over and draw through the loop on the hook.
chain space(s)	ch-sp(s)		The space beneath one or more chains.
double crochet	dc	× or +	Insert the hook into the next stitch and draw up a loop, yarn over and draw through both loops on the hook.
double crochet 2 together	dc2tog		(Insert the hook into the next stitch and draw up a loop) twice, yarn over and draw through all three loops on the hook.
double treble crochet	dtr		Yarn over twice, insert the hook into the next stitch and draw up a loop, (yarn over and draw through two loops on the hook) three times.
front loop	FL		The loop closest to you at the top of the stitch.
front post treble crochet	FPtr		Yarn over, insert the hook from the front to the back to the front around the post of the next stitch, yarn over and draw up a loop, (yarn over and draw through two loops) twice.
half treble crochet	htr		Yarn over, insert the hook into the next stitch and draw up a loop, yarn over and draw through all three loops on the hook.
repeat	rep		Replicate a series of given instructions.
skip	sk		Pass over a stitch or stitches – do not work into it.
slip stitch	ss/sl st	⬬ or ●	Insert the hook into the next stitch, draw up a loop through the stitch and the loop on the hook.
stitch(es)	st(s)		A group of one or more loops of yarn pulled through each other in a specified order until only 1 remains on the hook.
treble crochet	tr		Yarn over, insert the hook into the next stitch and draw up a loop, (yarn over and draw through two loops on the hook) twice.
treble crochet 2 together	tr2tog		Yarn over, insert the hook into the next stitch and draw up a loop, (yarn over and draw through two loops on the hook.
turning chain	t-ch		The chain made at the start of a row to bring your hook and yarn up to the height of the next row.
yarn over	yo		Pass the yarn over the hook so the yarn is caught in the throat of the hook.

If a pattern requires stitches that are not mentioned in this essentials section, stitch instructions will be given on the pattern page.

Crochet hooks

As well as coming in a variety of different sizes, crochet hooks come in a range of styles, too. With a bit of practice, you'll find the one that suits you

Different crochet hooks are designed with various factors in mind, from the type of project you will be working on to the level of grip and comfort required. Most importantly, crochet hooks come in different sizes, and the size of hook you use – while most of the time being determined by the weight of the yarn you are working with – will determine the look of your finished project. In general, the thicker the yarn you use the larger the crochet hook you will need, but using a large hook with a fine yarn can also produce an interesting, delicate fabric.

Crochet hooks are produced in different materials – mainly metal, wood and plastic – and some come with comfy-grip or ergonomic handles. Finding the right hook for you will most likely be a matter of trial and error, but as a beginner we recommend you work with a hook that is 5mm or larger, with Aran weight yarn. This will produce defined, easy-to-see stitches that will be simple to identify and work with.

"Finding the right hook for you will most likely be a matter of trial and error"

Anatomy of a crochet hook

There are six basic parts to a crochet hook, each with its own role in creating the stitches

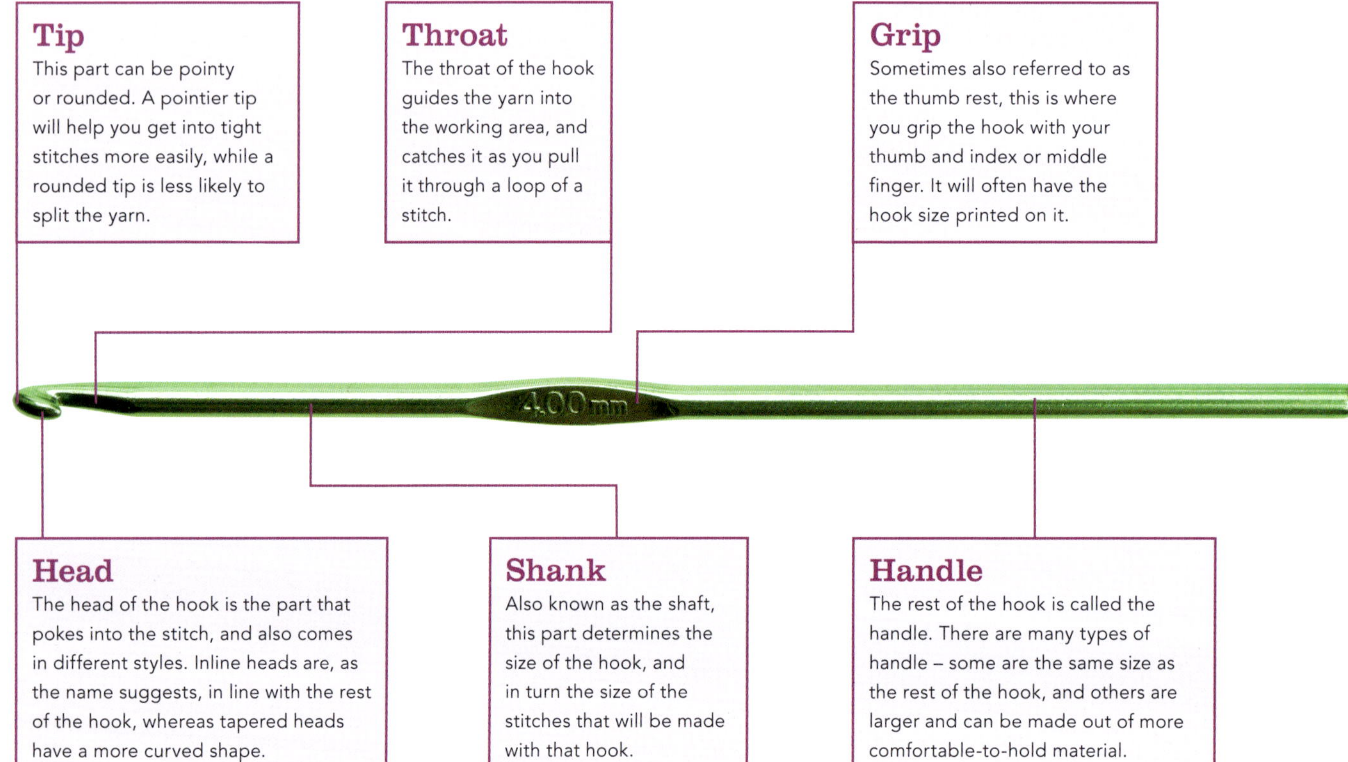

Hook sizes

Hook sizes are measured in millimetres, measured by the width across the shank. They are available from as small as 2mm to as large as 20mm or bigger. The size of hook you will need is related to the thickness of yarn that you use – thicker yarns need larger hooks – and will almost always be specified in a pattern.

Hooks can also be labelled in US sizes instead of in metric, with letters or numbers given to identify the size of the hook, as shown in the table below. If in doubt about the size of a particular hook, check the metric measurement, as this is less ambiguous.

UK size	US size
2mm, 2.25mm	B-1
2.5mm, 2.75mm	C-2
3mm, 3.25mm	D-3
3.5mm	E-4
3.75mm, 4mm	F-5
4mm, 4.25mm	G-6
4.5mm	G-7
5mm	H-8
5.5mm	I-9
6mm	J-10
6.5mm, 7mm	K-10.5
8mm	L-11
9mm	M-13
10mm	N,P-15

Hook materials

As well as varying in size and style, crochet hooks also come in a variety of materials, most commonly metal, plastic and wood – each with their own set of pros and cons. Aluminium hooks are smooth, strong and long lasting, but may feel uncomfortable in your hand after long periods of working. If you find you like the way a metal hook works with yarn but not the way it feels in your hand, you could try a metal hook with a rubber grip.

Plastic hooks are also smooth and easy to work with, but will bend more easily and could even snap. They can also make a squeaky noise when working the yarn, which could be off-putting to some. Most larger hooks are made of plastic so as to not be too heavy.

While wooden hooks feel warm to the touch, unlike cold aluminium hooks, and are flexible; they need to be well finished to ensure there are no rough spots that could snag yarn. They also need to be conditioned over time so they don't dry out. An alternative to wood is a hook made out of bamboo, which is lightweight, smooth and flexible, but prone to splintering.

To determine which type of hook is best for you, give each a try to see which feels best in your hand before you invest in multiple sizes.

Did you know?

The world's largest crochet hook was created by Jim Bolin in 2013, and is six foot 1.5 inches tall and three inches in diameter. Bolin also holds the record for the world's largest knitting needles and the world's largest golf tee.

Crochet kit bag

Although just a hook and a ball of yarn will get you pretty far in crochet, many other helpful tools are available

Case

You will only need a small case to keep all your crochet tools together, and ones designed with crochet tools in mind can be found at most craft stores. These will most likely be fitted with multiple elastic straps to keep your hooks and tools in place. However, as crochet hooks are only small, you could alternatively use a pencil case (as pictured) to keep everything in one place.

Row counter

Row counters are used for marking off how many rows you've worked. Just turn it once when you finish a row and it will keep track for you.

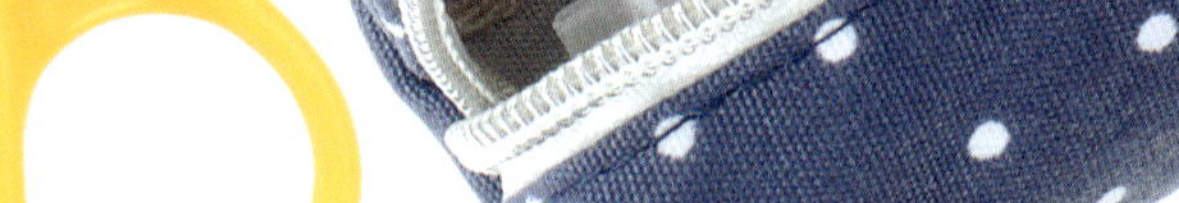

Scissors

A sharp pair of scissors is one of the most important tools a crocheter can keep to hand, as you will use them frequently for cutting yarn. Try to avoid using a blunt pair as this can cause yarn to fray, making it difficult to work with.

Yarn needles

Also called a tapestry needle or a darning needle, this handy tool will be useful for finishing off your projects neatly. As these needles are thick, blunt-tipped and have a large eye to fit the yarn into, they are the perfect tool for weaving in ends and stitching pieces together, giving a professional finish to your pieces.

Stitch markers

With multiple uses, stitch markers are some of the handiest tools a crocheter can keep in their kit bag. Their main purpose is to mark stitches. Place one in the first stitch of a row so you don't lose your place in a pattern.

Fibrefill

If you need to stuff your crochet projects you will need 'toy stuffing', also known as fibrefill. You can buy it in good craft stores or simply use the innards of an old pillow!

Crocheting stuffed toys is known as amigurumi, a Japanese word meaning knitted doll. Despite this, amigurumi toys are usually crocheted.

Safety eyes

To make sure that the toys you make are suitable for children, use safety eyes as they won't come out even when tugged on!

T-pins

These are essential if you are going to block your finished pieces. While any kind of sharp pin will work for blocking, T-pins are some of the easiest to work with as they are sturdy and long. It's important to check that you're buying rust-proof pins, or else your work could be quickly ruined by rust stains.

Tape measure

A measuring device is essential for checking your gauge (tension) when crocheting. A ruler will often do, but the flexibility of a tape measure makes it easier to use. A tape measure will also come in handy if you are crocheting something to exact measurements, like items of clothing.

Bright & beautiful blankets

Colourful crochet projects that are perfect for decorating the home

- ☐ EASY PEASY
- ☑ A BIT MORE TRICKY
- ☐ HARD-ISH
- ☐ QUITE A CHALLENGE

Easter blanket

With a gorgeous vintage colour palette, this blanket is the perfect project for Easter

Measurements

Complete blanket measures approximately 86 x 134cm (34 x 53in).

Materials

For complete blanket: 1 x 100g (295m) balls of Stylecraft Special DK (100% acrylic) in each of Lincoln (1834), Parma Violet (1724), Vintage Peach (1836), Cream (1005), Pistachio (1822), Pale Rose (1080), Buttermilk (1835), Duck Egg (1820), Blush (1833), Parchment (1218).
Size 5mm and 4mm crochet hooks; removable stitch markers (optional).

Tension

17 stitches and 10 rows, to 10 x 10cm (4 x 4in), over pattern, using 4mm hook.

Abbreviations

Ch, chain; **st(s)**, stitch(es); **dc**, double crochet; **tr**, treble crochet; **ch-sp**, chain space; **yrh**, yarn round hook; **ss**, slip stitch; **sp**, space; **bobble**, work 4tr bobble thus: yrh, [insert hook into st indicated, yrh, pull up loop, yrh, pull hook through first 2 loops on hook, leaving remaining loops on hook] 4 times (5 loops remain on hook), yrh and pull through all loops on hook; **cluster**, work 3tr cluster into ch-sp thus: yrh, [insert hook into ch-sp indicated, yrh, pull up loop, yrh, pull hook through first 2 loops on hook, leaving remaining loops on hook] 3 times (4 loops remain on hook), yrh and pull through all loops on hook; **cross4**, work crossed st thus: miss next st, 1tr in each of next 3 sts, yrh and work a long tr into missed st by inserting hook through missed st from front to back and drawing a long loop to not squash 3 tr and pull it across 3 tr, yrh and compete tr; **cross3**, work as cross4 over 3 sts (miss next st, 1tr in each of next 2 sts, work long tr in missed st).

Note

Starting chain is worked with a 5mm hook to prevent the 1st row from being too tight. If you prefer, place a removable stitch marker in every 20th ch on your foundation chain, to help keep track of counting.
On some rows, the last stitch of the row is the beginning 3ch from the previous row, which is always counted as a stitch. It is important to finish with a tr in the top of this 3ch as this will keep your edges straight and stitch count correct.
You may want to tick each numbered row off as you go along.
Unless stated otherwise, when changing colours, break off the current yarn. Weave in yarn tails as you go along. Yarn amounts are based on average requirements and are therefore approximate.
Instructions in square brackets are worked as stated after 2nd bracket.

To make

Foundation chain: With 5mm hook and Lincoln, make 121 ch. Change to 4mm hook.
1st row: 1dc in 2nd ch from hook, [1dc in next ch] to end, turn –120 sts.
2nd row: 1ch (does not count as a st throughout), [1dc in next st] to end, turn.
3rd row: 1ch, [1dc in next st] to end, turn.
4th row: As 3rd row, changing to Parma Violet on last yrh of last dc, turn.
5th and 6th rows: As 3rd row, changing to Vintage Peach on last yrh of last dc of 6th row.
7th and 8th rows: As 3rd row, changing to Cream on last yrh of last dc of 8th row.
9th and 10th rows: As 3rd row, changing to Pistachio on last yrh of last dc of 10th row.
11th row: 1st granny stripe row: 3ch (counts as 1tr throughout), 1tr in st at base of 3ch, [skip 2 sts, 3tr in next st] to last 2 sts, skip 1 st, 1tr in last st, turn.
12th row: 2nd granny stripe row: 3ch, 1tr in st at base of 3ch, [3tr in sp between next 2 3trgroups] to last 2 sts, skip 1 st, 1tr in last st, changing to Pale Rose on last yrh, turn.
13th row: 3ch (counts as 1tr throughout), skip st at base of 3ch, [1tr in next st] to end, turn.
14th row: 3ch, skip st at base of 3ch, [1tr in next st] to end, turn.
15th and 16th rows: As 14th row, changing to Buttermilk on last yrh of last tr of 16th row, turn.
17th to 20th rows: As 3rd row, changing to Duck Egg on last yrh of last dc of 20th row.
21st row: As 14th row.
22nd row: 1st v-stitch row: 3ch, skip st at base of 3ch, 2tr in next st, [skip next st, 2tr in next st] to last 2 sts, skip next st, 1tr in last st, turn.
23rd row: 2nd v-stitch row: 3ch, [2tr in sp between the 2 tr of next 2tr-group] to last

st, 1tr in last st, turn.
24th row: As 14th row, changing to Blush on last yrh of last tr.
25th to 28th rows: As 3rd row, changing to Parchment on last yrh of last dc of 28th row.
29th row: As 14th row.
30th and 31st rows: As 22nd and 23rd rows.
32nd row: As 14th row, changing to Lincoln on last yrh of last tr.
33rd to 36th rows: As 3rd row, changing to Parma Violet on last yrh of last dc of 36th row.
37th row: As 3rd row.
38th row: 1st bobble row: 1ch, bobble in same st, 1dc in next st, [bobble in next st, 1dc in next st] to end, turn.
39th row: As 3rd row, changing to Vintage Peach on last yrh of last dc.
40th to 43rd rows: As 3rd row, changing to Cream on last yrh of last dc of 43rd row.
44th row: As 11th row.
45th to 47th rows: As 12th row, changing to Pistachio on last yrh of last tr of 47th row.
48th and 49th rows: As 3rd row, changing to Pale Rose on last yrh of last dc of 49th row.
50th and 51st rows: As 3rd row, changing to Buttermilk on last yrh of last dc of 51st row.
52nd and 53rd rows: As 3rd row, changing to Duck Egg on last yrh of last dc of 53rd row.
54th and 55th rows: As 13th and 14th rows, changing to Blush on last yrh of last tr of 55th row.
56th row: As 22nd row.
57th and 58th rows: As 23rd row, changing to Parchment on last yrh of last tr of 58th row.
59th row: As 3rd row.
60th row: As 38th row.
61st row: As 3rd row, changing to Lincoln on last yrh of last dc.
62nd row: As 22nd row.
63rd and 64th rows: As 23rd row, changing to Parma Violet on last yrh of last tr of 64th row.
65th to 68th rows:
As 3rd row, changing to Vintage Peach on last yrh of last dc of 68th row.
69th row: 1st crossed row: 3ch, [cross4] to last 3 sts, cross3, turn.
70th row: As 3rd row.
71st and 72nd rows: As 69th and 70th rows, changing to Cream on last yrh of last dc of 72nd row.
73rd and 74th rows: As 3rd row, changing to Pistachio on last yrh of last dc of 7th row.
75th row: 1st cluster row: 3ch, skip next st, [1tr, 1ch, 1tr] in next st, *skip next 2 sts, [1tr, 1ch, 1tr] in next st; repeat from * to last 3 sts, skip next 2 sts, 1tr in last st, changing to Pale Rose on last yrh, turn.
76th row: 2nd cluster row: 5ch (counts as 1tr and 2ch), [cluster in next 1-ch-sp, 2ch] to last st, 1ch, 1tr in top of 3ch from previous row, changing to Cream on last yrh, turn.
77th row: 1ch (does not count as a st), 1dc in every cluster and in every ch, to 5ch of previous row, 1dc in each of next 3ch, turn.
78th row: As 3rd row, changing to Buttermilk on last yrh of last dc.
79th row: As 13th row.
80th to 82nd rows: As 14th row, changing to Duck Egg on last yrh of last tr of 82nd row.
83rd and 84th rows: As 11th and 12th rows, changing to Blush on last yrh of last tr of 84th row.
85th and 86th rows: As 12th row, changing to Parchment on last yrh of last tr of 86th row.
87th and 88th rows: As 12th row, changing to Lincoln on last yrh of last tr of 88th row. Do not fasten off.
Continue with 4mm hook and Lincoln – 120 sts.
89th row: 1ch (does not count as a st throughout), [1dc in next st] to end, turn.
90th to 92nd rows: As 89th row, changing to Parma Violet on last yrh of last dc of 92nd row.
93rd to 96th rows: As 89th row, changing to Vintage Peach on last yrh of last dc of 96th row.
97th row: As 89th row.
98th row: 1st Bobble row: 1ch, bobble in same st, 1dc in next st, [bobble in next st, 1dc in next st] to end, turn.
99th row: As 89th row.
100th and 101st rows: As 98th and 99th rows, changing to Cream on last yrh of last dc of 101st row.
102nd to 105th rows: As 89th row, changing to Pistachio on last yrh of last dc of 105th row.
106th to 109th rows: As 89th row, changing to Pale Rose on last yrh of last dc of 109th row.
110th row: 3ch, skip st at base of 3ch, [1tr in next st] to end, turn.
111th row: 1st V-stitch row: 3ch, skip st at base of 3ch, 2tr in next st, [skip next st, 2tr in next st] to last 2 sts, skip next st, 1tr in last st, turn.
112th row: 2nd V-stitch row: 3ch, [2tr in sp between the 2 tr of next 2tr-gp] to last st, 1tr in last st, turn.
113th row: As 110th row, changing to Buttermilk on last yrh of last tr. 1
114th row: As 89th row.
115th row: 1st crossed row: 3ch, [cross4] to last 3 sts, cross3, turn. crochet
116th row: As 89th row.
117th and 118th rows: As 115th and 116th rows, changing to Duck Egg on last yrh of last dc of 118th row.
119th to 121st rows: As 110th to 112th rows.
122nd row: As 110th row, changing to Blush on last yrh of last tr.
123rd to 126th rows: As 89th row, changing to Parchment on last yrh of last dc of 126th row.
127th to 129th rows: As 89th row, changing to Lincoln on last yrh of last dc of 129th row.
130th row: 1st Cluster row: 3ch, skip next st, [1tr, 1ch, 1tr] in next st, *skip next 2 sts, [1tr, 1ch, 1tr] in next st; repeat from * to last 3 sts, skip next 2 sts, 1tr in last st, changing to Parma Violet on last yrh, turn.
131st row: 2nd Cluster row: 5ch (counts as 1tr and 2ch), [cluster in next 1-ch-sp, 2ch] to last st, 1ch, 1tr in top of 3ch from previous row, changing to Parchment on last yrh, turn.
132nd row: 1ch (does not count as a st), 1dc in every cluster and in every ch, to 5ch of previous row, 1dc in each of next 3ch, turn.
133rd to 134th rows: As 89th row, changing to Vintage Peach on last yrh of last dc of 134th row.
135th and 136th rows: As 111th and 112th rows, changing to Cream on last yrh of last tr of 136th row.
137th and 138th rows: As 112th row, changing to Pistachio on last yrh of last tr of 138th row.
139th and 140th rows: As 112th row, changing to Pale Rose on last yrh of last tr of 140th row.
141st row: As 89th row.
142nd row: As 98th row.
143rd row: As 89th row, changing to

Buttermilk on last yrh of last dc.

144th row: 3ch, skip st at base of 3ch, [1tr in next st] to end, turn.

145th row: 3ch, skip st at base of 3ch, [1tr in next st] to end, changing to Duck Egg on last yrh of last tr, turn.

146th and 147th rows: As 144th and 145th rows, changing to Blush on last yrh of last tr of 147th row.

148th to 151st rows: As 89th row, changing to Parchment on last yrh of last dc of 151st row.

152nd row: 1st granny stripe row: 3ch, 1tr in st at base of 3ch, [skip 2 sts, 3tr in next st] to last 2 sts, skip 1 st, 1tr in last st, turn.

153rd row: 2nd granny stripe row: 3ch, 1tr in st at base of 3ch, [3tr in sp between next 2 3tr-groups] to last 2 sts, skip 1 st, 1tr in last st, changing to Lincoln on last yrh, turn.

154th and 155th rows: As 89th row, changing to Parma Violet on last yrh of last dc of 155th row.

156th and 157th rows: As 89th row, changing to Vintage Peach on last yrh of last dc of 157th row.

158th and 159th rows: As 89th row, changing to Cream on last yrh of last dc of 159th row.

160th and 161st rows: As 89th row, changing to Pistachio on last yrh of last dc of 161st row.

162nd row: As 144th row.

163rd to 165th rows: As 145th row, changing to Pale Rose on last yrh of last tr of 165th row.

166th to 169th rows: As 89th row. Fasten off.

Border

When working the border, especially along the row ends, work a section at a time and check your tension. If your work is too tight and pulling, add a few more trebles, evenly spaced; if your work is wavy and loose, decrease the number of trebles along the sides, evenly spaced. Unless stated otherwise, when changing colours, break off the current yarn.

With 4mm hook and Buttermilk, hold blanket with Lincoln foundation ch uppermost and join yarn with ss to top-right corner. Work along spare loops of foundation chain and work in rounds that are joined.

1st round: 3ch (counts as 1tr throughout), skip st at base of 3ch, *[1tr in next st] to next corner, work [2tr, 2ch, 2tr] in corner st, [1tr in each dc row-end and 2tr in each tr row-end] to next corner, work 3tr in corner st; repeat from * once more, ss in top of beginning 3ch. Fasten off Buttermilk.

2nd round: Join Cream with a ss, to st to left of top-right corner st, 1ch (does not count as a st throughout), 1dc in same st at base of 1ch, *[1dc in next st] to next corner, work [2dc, 2ch, 2dc] in corner st; repeat from * to end, ss in first dc. Fasten off Cream.

3rd and 4th rounds: Join Lincoln with a ss to st to left of top-right corner st. Work as given for 2nd round. Fasten off Lincoln.

5th round: Join Vintage Peach with a ss to st to left of top-right corner st, 3ch (counts as 1tr), skip st at base of 3ch, [1tr in next st] to corner, [2tr, 2ch, 2tr] in corner st; repeat from * to end, ss in top of beginning 3ch.
Fasten off Vintage Peach.

6th and 7th rounds: Join Duck Egg with a ss to st to left of top-right corner st. Work as given for 2nd round.
Fasten off Duck Egg.

8th round: Join Cream with a ss to st to left of top-right corner st. Work as given for 2nd round.
Fasten off Cream.

9th round: Join Parma Violet with a ss to st to left of top-right corner st. Work as given for 5th round.

10th round: With Parma Violet, work as given for 2nd round.
Fasten off Parma Violet.

Edging round: With wrong side facing, join Parchment with a ss to any st, 3ch (not counted as a st), 1tr in same st at base of beginning 3ch, [ss in next st, 1tr in next st] to end, ss into top of beginning 3ch.
Fasten off and neaten your final tails.

☐ EASY PEASY
☑ A BIT MORE TRICKY
☐ HARD-ISH
☐ QUITE A CHALLENGE

Technicolour floral blanket

This floral blanket is a wonderful project to get stuck into during dark winter evenings, where you can dream of summer gardens!

Measurements

Complete blanket measures 82 x 138cm (32.3 x 54.3in).

Materials

For complete blanket: 4 x 50g (92m) balls of Stylecraft Classique Cotton DK (100% cotton) in each of Fondant (3094) and Peppermint (3691), 3 in each of Lavender (3673), Shrimp (3674), Soft Lime (3663), Sunflower (3662) and Sky Blue (3667), 2 in each of Greek Blue (3095) and Busy Lizzie (3657). Size 3mm crochet hook.

Tension

1 motif measures 10cm (4in) on size 3mm hook.

Abbreviations

Ch, chain; **dc**, double crochet; **tr**, treble; **htr**, half treble; **ss**, slip stitch; **ch-sp**, chain space; **st(s)**, stitch(es); **yrh**, yarn round hook.

Note

Yarn amounts are based on average requirements and are therefore approximate. Instructions in square brackets are worked as stated after 2nd bracket.

To make hexagon motif

In total make 12 in each of the motif colourways of 1, 2, 6, 8, 9 and 10 and 13 in each of the motif colourways of 3, 4, 5, 7, 11 and 12 (see list below).

Foundation: Wrap yarn round index finger once, leave a generous tail, insert hook into yarn around finger, yrh, pull a loop through, 1ch (does not count as st), 12dc into ring, ss to first dc to join.

1st round: 4ch, (counts as 1tr, 1ch), [1tr in next st, 1ch] 11 times, ss in 3rd of 4ch, fasten off – 12 sts.

2nd round: Join in 2nd colour in any ch-sp, 3ch, 2tr in next tr, 3ch, ss in same tr (this forms 1 petal), ss in next ch-sp, [3ch, 2tr in next tr, 3ch, ss in same tr, ss in next ch-sp] 11 times, fasten off after last ss – 12 petals.

3rd round: Join 3rd colour to 2nd tr (counting from right) of any petal, of any petal, 1ch, 1dc in same place, 4ch, [1dc in top of next petal, 4ch] 11 times, ss to first dc at beg of round – 12 ch-sp.

4th round: Ss twice in next ch-sp, 1ch, 1dc in same place, 5ch, [1dc in next ch-sp, 5ch] 11 times, ss to first dc – 12 ch-sp.

5th round: Ss in next ch-sp, 1ch, *(2dc, 1htr, 3tr) in next ch-sp, 3ch, (3tr, 1htr, 2dc) in next ch-sp; repeat from * 5 times more, ending ss in dc at start of round. Fasten off.

Motif colourways

Beginning with centre colour:

1: Lavender, Sky Blue, Shrimp
2: Shrimp, Lavender, Busy Lizzie
3: Greek Blue, Fondant, Lavender
4: Lavender, Sunflower, Fondant
5: Peppermint, Lavender, Soft Lime
6: Soft Lime, Shrimp, Fondant
7: Sunflower, Soft Lime, Peppermint
8: Busy Lizzie, Peppermint, Sunflower
9: Peppermint, Busy Lizzie, Greek Blue
10: Shrimp, Sky Blue, Soft Lime
11: Sky Blue, Greek Blue, Peppermint
12: Fondant, Sunflower, Sky Blue

Joining motifs

Following motif sequence (right): All motifs are joined at ch-sp intervals. Complete first half of petal on last round, 1ch, ss to ch-sp of motif to be joined, 1ch, complete second half of petal. Where there are more than 2 motifs joining together, work a ss then 1ch in appropriate ch-sp. Once complete, sew in all ends using tapestry needle.

Motif sequence

Row A: 12, 7, 4, 11, 6, 7, 8, 5, 9, 4, 1, 12, 2, 10, 8
Row B: 2, 10, 3, 5, 2, 3, 1, 4, 11, 1, 7, 4, 5, 6, 9
Row C: 9, 4, 2, 7, 4, 9, 7, 2, 3, 12, 9, 11, 8, 11, 6
Row D: 4, 8, 11, 6, 1, 5, 3, 12, 5, 7, 10, 3, 6, 12, 1
Row E: 10, 2, 3, 10, 11, 6, 10, 11, 8, 6, 8, 9, 5, 3, 7
Row F: 1, 7, 5, 12, 8, 9, 12, 4, 2, 9, 7, 5, 1, 4, 10
Row G: 9, 1, 9, 6, 2, 5, 11, 10, 12, 5, 2, 7, 12, 8, 11
Row H: 6, 12, 7, 8, 11, 3, 1, 9, 8, 1, 3, 10, 3, 5, 6
Row I: 3, 5, 2, 4, 12, 7, 10, 6, 11, 4, 12, 9, 11, 8, 2
Row J: 1, 11, 6, 10, 8, 3, 4, 2, 12, 10, 3, 5, 1, 4, 7

To finish

Weave in ends.

Feel-good throw

Crochet a cluster of colourful puffs for a luxurious, textured blanket from Anita Mundt

- ☐ EASY PEASY
- ☐ A BIT MORE TRICKY
- ☑ HARD-ISH
- ☐ QUITE A CHALLENGE

To make

You can't beat a tactile blanket for snuggling up in, and this throw is no exception. Each flower is worked with two strands so you can easily swap the colour of one strand at a time – a canny way to create a subtle ombre effect.

As you use two strands of yarn throughout, you may need to split some of your balls of yarn before you start. Alternatively, work one strand from the middle of the ball, and the other from the outside.

Start each flower by choosing the colours. You need between four and six colours for each flower. Call the darkest one yarn A, and use this to start. From round 2 onwards, change one strand each round to create a graduating effect, going from darker shades to lighter. Have fun and play with the colour changes as you work to create your own unique throw.

How many hexagons?

Make 39 hexagons and 6 half hexagons in total.
Make 26 hexagons using 2 strands of Aconite yarn for the last 2 rounds, creating the light mustard surround.
Make 10 hexagons using 1 strand of Aconite and 1 strand of Nutmeg yarn, creating the medium mustard surround.
Make 3 hexagons using 2 strands of Nutmeg yarn, creating the dark mustard surround.
Make 6 half hexagons using 2 strands of Aconite throughout.

Hexagon

Using 2 strands of yarn A.
Foundation: Ch4, join to 1st ch with a ss to make a ring.
Round 1: 6dc in the ring, join to top of 1st dc with a ss.
Round 2: Break off 1 strand of yarn A and replace with a lighter yarn. Ch3 (counts as 1st tr), make one 5tr petal popcorn in each stitch with ch3 between each. Join to the top of the 1st petal popcorn with a ss.
Round 3: Break off 1 strand of dark yarn and replace with 1 strand of lighter yarn. Ss into 1st 3ch-sp, ch3 (counts as 1st tr), make two 5tr petal popcorns in each 3ch-sp with a ch3 between each petal popcorn. Join to the top of the 1st petal popcorn with a ss. (12 3ch-sps)
Round 4: Break off 1 strand of dark yarn and replace with 1 strand of lighter yarn. Ss into 1st 3ch-sp, ch3 (counts as 1st tr), *make 1 x 6tr petal popcorn in the 1st 3ch-sp, ch3, (1 x 6tr petal popcorn, ch3, 1

Measurements

The throw is 120 x 110cm (47.2 x 43.3in). Each hexagon is 20cm (7.8in) across when blocked.

Materials

For complete blanket: Holst Garn Coast, 55% merino lambswool/45% cotton, 50g (350m) ball, or you can use a similar 4ply weight yarn
50g balls: 5 in Aconite (CO13), 3 x Robins Egg (CO28), 2 x Nimbus (CO26), 2 x Sky Light (CO25), 2 x Kingfisher (CO29), 2 x Harbour (CO30), 1 x Nutmeg (CO08), 1 x Tweed (CO27), 1 x Porcelain (CO31), 1 x Redcurrant (CO46), 1 x Plum (CO47), 1 x Cassis (CO48)
25g balls: 1 x Denim (CO34), 1 x Warm brown (CO16)
3mm crochet hook.
Tapestry needle.

Abbreviations

ch, chain; **ch-sp**, chain space; **dc**, double crochet; **htr**, half treble **tr**, treble; **ss**, slip stitch; **st(s)**, stitch(es).

Special stitches

Petal popcorn.

HOW TO STITCH A PETAL POPCORN

The centre flowers are made up of petals of different sizes. The petal is a popcorn st. Some are made with 5 treble sts, some with 6 and some with 8. All the petals, whatever size, are made in the following way: 5 (6 or 8) tr into the same st, take hook out of the loop left on your hook, place it back into the top of the 1st treble loop and then back into the dropped loop. With 2 loops on your hook, yarn over hook and pull the yarn though both the loops. Pull tightly to curl your trebles into a petal. For the first petal of each row substitute the 1st tr with ch3.

x 6tr petal popcorn) all in next 3ch-sp, ch3; repeat from * 5 times (6 times in total). Join to the top of the 1st petal popcorn with a ss. (18 3ch-sps)
Round 5: Break off 1 strand of dark yarn and replace with 1 strand of lighter yarn. Ss into 1st 3ch-sp, ch3 (counts as 1st tr), *make 1 x 6tr petal popcorn in the 3ch-sp, ch3, (1 x 6tr petal popcorn, ch3, 1 x 6tr petal popcorn) all in next 3ch-sp, ch3; repeat from * 8 times (9 times in total). Join to the top of the 1st petal popcorn with a ss. (27 3ch-sps).
Round 6: Break off 1 strand of dark yarn and replace with 1 strand of lighter yarn. Ss into 1st 3ch-sp, ch3 (counts as 1st tr), *(make 1 x 8tr petal popcorn, ch3, 1 x 8tr petal popcorn) all in the next 3ch-sp, ch3, (make 1 x 8tr petal popcorn, ch3) in each of the next 8 3ch-sps; repeat from * 2 times (3 times in total). Join to the top of the 1st petal popcorn with a ss.
(30 3ch-sps)
Break off both strands of yarn and pull to the back of the work.
Round 7: Join 2 strands of your mustard coloured yarn in any 3ch-sp. In this round we will always work in the 3ch-sps.
*[Ch3 (counts as 1st tr) 2tr, ch2, 3tr] in the same 3ch-sp.
3htr in next 3ch-sp.
3dc in next 3ch-sp.
3dc in next 3ch-sp.
3htr in next 3ch-sp; repeat from * 5 times (6 times in total).
Join in the top of the 1st tr with a ss.
Round 8: Ch3 (counts as 1st tr), 1tr into each st around, and (1tr, ch1, 1tr) in each 2ch-sp. Join in the top of the 1st tr with a ss.

Half hexagon

This motif is made in rows, so turn your work at the end of each row.
Using two strands of Aconite:
Foundation: Ch20.
Row 1: Ch3 (counts as 1st tr), 1tr into st at base of ch3, work 1tr into each st along but 2tr in the last st.
Row 2: Ch3 (counts as 1st tr), 1tr into st at base of ch3, 2tr in next st, work 1tr into each st until the last 2 sts, work 2tr in each of the last 2 sts.
Row 3: As row 1.
Row 4: As row 2.
Row 5: As row 1.
Row 6: As row 2.
Rows 7, 8 and 9: As row 1.

Break off yarn and pull to back of work.

To make up

Wet block all pieces and leave to air dry. Join the hexagons by holding the right sides together and dc along the edge (this gives a dc seam on the wrong side), use 2 strands of mustard yarn to do this.

The throw has 7 rows. Start with the centre row: Join the 3 hexagons with the dark mustard surrounds together in a row, then join one hexagon with a medium mustard surround on each end.
The row on each side of the centre row consists of 4 medium mustard hexagons in the centre with a light mustard hexagon on each side.
The final 2 rows on each side are made up of all light mustard-coloured hexagons.
Fill the spaces along the edges with the half hexagons leaving a zigzag edge at the top and bottom.
Finally, do a row of htr down the straight sides to neaten the edge.
Sew in all loose ends with a tapestry needle.

ANITA MUNDT

Anita studied textile design while she was at university in Yorkshire. Although she no longer works in the textile industry, creating with textiles is very much in her heart. She now lives in an old village school, which she is slowly renovating with her husband.

- ☐ EASY PEASY
- ☑ A BIT MORE TRICKY
- ☐ HARD-ISH
- ☐ QUITE A CHALLENGE

Vintage blanket

This elegant and timeless design is the perfect project to cosy up with

CREATE STRIPS OF CROCHET SQUARES TO MAKE THIS DELICATE BED COVER

Measurements

Approximately 180 x 180cm (71 x 71in), excluding edging.

Materials

14 x 100g (212m) balls of Sirdar Cotton DK (100% cotton) in Light Taupe (504).
Size 3mm crochet hook.

Tension

For each individual square, 1st to 13th rows measure 16 x 16cm (6 x 6in), using 3mm hook.

Abbreviations

Ch, chain; **dc**, double crochet; **tr**, treble crochet; **ss**, slip stitch; **sp**, space; **ch-sp(s)**, chain space(s).

Note

Yarn amounts are based on average requirements and are therefore approximate.
Instructions in square brackets are worked as stated after 2nd bracket.

First strip

First square: With 3mm hook, make 44ch.

1st row (right side): 1tr in 8th ch from hook (counts as 1tr, 2-ch-sp, 1tr), [2ch, miss next 2 ch, 1tr in next ch] to end, turn – 13 ch-sps.

2nd row: 5ch (counts as 1tr and 2ch throughout), miss first ch-sp, 1tr in next tr, *2ch, miss next ch-sp, 1tr in next tr*; repeat from * to * 4 times more, 2tr in next ch-sp, 1tr in next tr, repeat from * to * 5 times, 2ch, miss next 2 ch, 1tr in next ch, turn.

3rd row: 5ch, miss first ch-sp, 1tr in next tr, *2ch, miss next ch-sp, 1tr in next tr*; repeat from * to * 4 times more, 1tr in each of next 3 tr, repeat from * to * 5 times, 2ch, miss next 2 ch, 1tr in next ch, turn.

4th row: 5ch, miss first ch-sp, 1tr in next tr, *2ch, miss next ch-sp, 1tr in next tr*; repeat from * to * twice more, [2tr in next ch-sp, 1tr in next tr] twice, 2ch, miss next 2 tr, 1tr in next tr, [2tr in next ch-sp, 1tr in next tr] twice, repeat from * to * 3 times, 2ch, miss 2 ch, 1tr in next ch, turn.

5th row: 5ch, miss first ch-sp, 1tr in next tr, *2ch, miss next ch-sp, 1tr in next tr*; repeat from * to * once more, 2tr in next ch-sp, 1tr in next tr, 2ch, miss next 2 tr, 1tr in each of next 4 tr, 5ch, miss next ch-sp, 1tr in each of next 4 tr, 2ch, miss next 2 tr, 1tr in next tr, 2tr in next ch-sp, 1tr in next tr, repeat from * to * twice, 2ch, miss next 2 ch, 1tr in next ch, turn.

6th row: 5ch, miss first ch-sp, 1tr in next tr, *2ch, miss next ch-sp, 1tr in next tr*; repeat from * to * once more, 1tr in each of next 3 tr, 2tr in next ch-sp, 1tr in next tr, 5ch, miss next 3 tr, 1dc in next ch-sp, 5ch, miss next 3 tr, 1tr in next tr, 2tr in next ch-sp, 1tr in each of next 4 tr, repeat from * to * twice, 2ch, miss next 2 ch, 1tr in next ch, turn.

7th row: 5ch, miss first ch-sp, 1tr in next tr, [2tr in next ch-sp, 1tr in next tr] twice, 2ch, miss next 2 tr, 1tr in next tr, 5ch, miss next 3 tr, [1dc in next ch-sp, 5ch] twice, miss next 3 tr, 1tr in next tr, 2ch, miss next 2 tr, 1tr in next tr, [2tr in next ch-sp, 1tr in next tr] twice, 2ch, miss next 2 ch, 1tr in next ch, turn.

8th row: 5ch, miss first ch-sp, 1tr in next tr, *2ch, miss next 2 tr, 1tr in next tr*; repeat from * to * once more, 2tr in next ch-sp, 1tr in next tr, 3tr in next ch-sp, 5ch, 1dc in next ch-sp, 5ch, 3tr in next ch-sp, 1tr in next tr, 2tr in next ch-sp, 1tr in next tr, repeat from * to * twice, 2ch, miss next 2 ch, 1tr in next ch, turn.

9th row: 5ch, miss first ch-sp, 1tr in next tr, *2ch, miss next ch-sp, 1tr in next tr*; repeat from * to * once more, 1tr in each of next 3 tr, 2ch, miss next 2 tr, 1tr in next tr, 3tr in next ch-sp, 2ch, 3tr in next ch-sp, 1tr in next tr, 2ch, miss next 2 tr, 1tr in each of next 4 tr, repeat from * to * twice, 2ch, miss next 2 ch, 1tr in next ch, turn.

10th row: 5ch, miss first ch-sp, 1tr in next tr, *2ch, miss next ch-sp, 1tr in next tr*; repeat from * to * once more, 2ch, miss next 2 tr, 1tr in next tr, 2tr in next ch-sp, 1tr in each of next 4 tr, 2ch, miss next ch-sp, 1tr in each of next 4 tr, 2tr in next ch-sp, 1tr in next tr, 2ch, miss next 2 tr, 1tr in next tr, repeat from * to * twice, 2ch, miss next 2 ch, 1tr in next ch, turn.

11th row: 5ch, miss first ch-sp, 1tr in next tr, *2ch, miss next ch-sp, 1tr in next tr*; repeat from * to * twice more, [2ch, miss next 2 tr, 1tr in next tr] twice, 2tr in next ch-sp, 1tr in next tr, [2ch, miss next 2 tr, 1tr in next tr] twice, repeat from * to * 3 times, 2ch, miss next 2 ch, 1tr in next ch, turn.

12th row: As 3rd row.

13th row: 5ch, miss first ch-sp, 1tr in next tr, *2ch, miss next ch-sp, 1tr in next tr*; repeat from * to * 4 times more, 2ch, miss next 2 tr, 1tr in next tr, repeat from *

to * 5 times, 2ch, miss next 2 ch, 1tr in next ch, do not turn. ***

Edging round: 8ch (counts as 1tr and 5ch), 4tr in first corner sp, *2ch, miss next sp, [4tr in next sp, 2ch, miss next sp] 5 times**, [4tr, 5ch, 4tr] all in next corner sp*; repeat from * to * twice more, then repeat from * to ** once more, 3tr in corner sp at beginning of round, ss in 3rd ch of beginning 8ch. Fasten off.

Second square: Work as given for first square to ***.

Joining round: With wrong sides together, matching pattern so the 13th rows are aligned and facing in the same direction and with second square in front of first square, join one side edge of squares thus, 5ch (counts as 1tr and 2ch), ss in ch-sp at corner of first square, 2ch, 4tr in corner sp of second square, [1ch, ss in next ch-sp of first square, 1ch, miss next sp of second square and work 4tr in following sp] 6 times, 2ch, ss in ch-sp at corner of first square, 2ch, 4tr in same corner sp of second square, complete second square in the same way as given on edging round of first square, ending with 3tr in corner sp at beginning of round, ss in 3rd ch of beginning 5ch. Fasten off.

Make a further 8 squares and join them in the same way as the second square was joined to the first, thus making the first strip 10 squares wide.

Second strip

11th square: Work as given for first square to ***.

Joining round: Work as edging round of first square to **, 4tr in next corner sp, 2ch, then with wrong sides together, having 11th square in front of first square of first strip and with 13th row of squares at bottom, join these edges thus, ss in ch-sp at corner of first square, 2ch, 4tr in corner sp of 11th square, [1ch, ss in next ch-sp of first square, 1ch, miss next sp of 11th square and work 4tr in following sp] 6 times, 2ch, ss in corner join on first strip, 2ch, 4tr in same corner sp of 11th square, complete 11th square in the same way as given on edging round of first square, ending with: 3tr in corner sp at beginning of round, ss in 3rd ch of beginning 8ch. Fasten off.

12th square: Work as given for first square to ***.

Joining round: With wrong sides together, 13th row aligned and 12th square in front of 11th square, join edges thus, 5ch (counts as 1tr and 2ch), ss in ch-sp at corner on 11th square, 2ch, 4tr in corner sp on 12th square, *[1ch, ss in next ch-sp on 11th square, 1ch, miss next sp on 11th square and work 4tr in following sp] 6 times, 2ch, ss in corner join, 2ch, 4tr in same corner sp on 12th square*; repeat from * to * once, joining to second square of first strip, then complete 12th square in the same way as given on edging round of first square, ending with 3tr in corner sp at beginning of round, ss in 3rd ch of beginning 5ch. Fasten off. Make a further 8 squares and join them in the same way as the 12th square was joined to the 11th square and to the first strip.

Third to tenth strips

Make and join a further 8 strips in the same way, thus making the bedspread 10 squares long and 10 squares wide.

Edging

With right side facing, and with 3mm hook, join yarn to any corner ch-sp, 3ch (counts as 1tr), **work [1tr, [5ch, ss in 3rd ch from hook (a picot made here and throughout), 2ch, 2tr] 3 times] all in same corner ch-sp, [miss next 4 tr, work [2tr, 5ch, ss in 3rd ch from hook, 2ch, 2tr] all in next sp] 6 times, *work [2tr, 5ch, ss in 3rd ch from hook, 2ch, 2tr] all in next join, [miss next 4 tr, work [2tr, 5ch, ss in 3rd ch from hook, 2ch, 2tr] all in next sp] 6 times*; repeat from * to * to next corner ch-sp, work 1tr in corner ch-sp**, work from ** to ** 3 times more, omitting 1tr at end of last repeat, ss in 3rd ch of beginning 3ch.

Fasten off and neaten ends. Press according to ball band.

- ☐ EASY PEASY
- ☑ A BIT MORE TRICKY
- ☐ HARD-ISH
- ☐ QUITE A CHALLENGE

Heart blanket

Create this stunning patchwork-style blanket with a distinctive heart motif

Measurements

Complete blanket will measure approximately 55 x 65cm (21½ x 25½in).

Materials

1 x 50g (175m) ball of Wendy Merino 4ply (100% wool) in each of Birch (2365), Coulis (2408), Carnation (2384), Pewter (2400) and Saffron (2399).
Size 3mm crochet hook.

Tension

Each motif measures approximately 11 x 11cm 4½ x 4½in), using 3mm hook and 4ply yarn.

Abbreviations

Ch, chain; **st(s)**, stitch(es); **ss**, slip stitch; **tr**, treble crochet; **ch-sp**, chain space; **dtr**, double treble crochet; **htr**, half treble crochet; **yrh**, yarn round hook; **dc2tog**, double crochet 2 sts together (to decrease 1 st) thus: [insert hook into next st or space as indicated, yrh, and pull through] twice, yrh and pull through all 3 loops on hook; **ttr**, triple treble crochet.

Note

Yarn amounts are based on average requirements and are therefore approximate. Instructions in square brackets are worked as stated after 2nd bracket.

Heart motif

With recommended hook and first colour, make 5ch, ss in first ch to form a ring.

1st round: 3ch (counts as 1tr here and throughout instructions), 2tr into ring, 3ch, [3tr into ring, 3ch] 3 times, ss in top of beginning 3ch.

2nd round: 3ch, 1tr in each of next 2 tr, *[2tr, 3ch, 2tr] in next corner 3ch-sp, 1tr in each of next 3 tr; repeat from * twice more, [2tr, 3ch, 2tr] in last corner 3ch-sp, ss in top of beginning 3ch. Fasten off and rejoin same yarn with a ss to any corner 3ch-sp.

3rd round (part round): *2ch, miss next 3 tr, [1dtr, 2ch] 6 times in next tr, miss next 3 tr, ss in next corner 3ch-sp; repeat from * once more.

4th round: 3ch, 1tr in each of next 7 sts, 3tr in next corner 3ch-sp (point of heart made), 1tr in each of next 7 sts, 1tr in next 3ch-sp, [2tr in next 2ch-sp, 1tr in next dtr] 5 times, 2htr in next 2ch-sp, 1dc in next dtr, dc2tog across next two 2ch-sps (thus missing the ss), 1dc in next dtr, 2htr in next 2ch-sp, [1tr in next dtr, 2tr in next 2ch-sp] 5 times, ss in top of beginning 3ch – 56 sts. Fasten off.

5th round (in back loops only): Holding heart upside down, join second colour with a ss to first tr in point of heart, [3ch, miss next st, 1dc in next st] to end, 3ch, ss in base of beginning 3ch – 28 ch-sps and 28 dc.

6th round: Ss in next 3ch-sp, now working only in 3ch-sps, work thus: 1ch (counts as 1dc), 2dc in same 3ch-sp, 3tr in next 3ch-sp, 3dtr in next 3ch-sp, 3ttr in next 3ch-sp, 3ch (corner made), 3ttr in next 3ch-sp, 3dtr in next 3ch-sp, 3tr in next 3ch-sp, 3htr in next 3ch-sp, 3dc in next 3ch-sp, 3htr in next 3ch-sp, 3tr in next 3ch-sp, 3ch (corner made), [3tr in next 3ch-sp] 3 times, 3dtr in next 3ch-sp (centre top of heart), [3tr in next 3ch-sp] 3 times, 3ch (corner made), 3tr in next 3ch-sp, 3htr in next 3ch-sp, 3dc in next 3ch-sp, 3htr in next 3ch-sp, 3tr in next 3ch-sp, 3dtr in next 3ch-sp, 3ttr in next 3ch-sp, 3ch (corner made), 3ttr in next 3ch-sp, 3dtr in next 3ch-sp, 3tr in next 3ch-sp, ss in beginning 1ch – 84 sts and 4 corner 3ch-sps.

7th round: 3ch, work 1tr in each st and [2tr, 3ch, 2tr] in each corner 3ch-sp, ss in top of beginning 3ch. Fasten off.

Heart blanket

Work 1 heart motif in each of the following colour combinations:

First colour Saffron, second colour Birch. First colour Saffron, second colour Coulis. First colour Saffron, second colour Pewter. First colour Coulis, second colour Pewter. First colour Coulis, second colour Birch. First colour Carnation, second colour Saffron. First colour Carnation, second colour Coulis. First colour Birch, second colour Pewter. First colour Birch, second colour Carnation. First colour Pewter, second colour Carnation.

Then make another 10 motifs, reversing all of the above colours. Sew motifs together in 5 rows of 4 squares, using the photo as a guide, or in any order of your choice.

Blanket edging

1st round: Join Birch to any corner 3ch-sp, 3ch (counts as 1tr), [1tr, 3ch, 2tr] in same corner sp, *[1tr in next st] to next corner 3ch-sp, [2tr, 3ch, 2tr] in corner 3ch-sp; repeat from * twice more, [1tr in next st] to end, ss in top of beginning 3ch. Fasten off. Repeat 1st round with each of the remaining 4 colours, in the following order: Pewter, Saffron, Carnation, and finally, Coulis.

Fasten off and weave in ends. Press according to ball band.

In full bloom

Crochet a stunning throw and matching cushion for your home or garden

- ☐ EASY PEASY
- ☑ A BIT MORE TRICKY
- ☐ HARD-ISH
- ☐ QUITE A CHALLENGE

Measurements

Blanket: Approximately 88 x 116cm (34½ x 45¾in).
Cushion: Approximately 30 x 30cm (12 x 12in).

Materials

Stylecraft Special DK (100% acrylic), 100g (295m) balls; 1 ball in Walnut (1054) and 2 balls in each of Gold (1709), Dandelion (1856), Citron (1263), Greengage (1124) and White (1001).
A 4mm crochet hook.
32 x 32cm (12½ x 12½in) square of fabric for cushion back; 30 x 30cm (12 x 12in) square cushion insert.
Sewing needle and thread for making up cushion.

Tension

Each motif measures approx 14 x 14cm (5½ x 5½), using Stylecraft Special DK and 4mm hook.

Abbreviations

ch(s), chain(s); **ch-sp**, chain space; **dc**, double crochet; **dtr**, double treble crochet; **htr**, half treble crochet; **tr**, treble crochet; **5tr-cl**, 5 treble cluster to make a bobble thus: [yrh, insert hook in st, yrh and pull loop through, yrh and pull through first 2 loops only] 5 times all in same st (6 loops on hook), yrh and pull through all 6 loops to complete bobble: **ss**, slip stitch; **sp**, space; **st(s)**, stitch(es); **yrh**, yarn round hook.

Note

The last round of each square is worked using a join-as-you-go method (explained in pattern), so that there is no sewing up at the end. Yarn amounts are based on average requirements and are therefore approximate. Instructions in square brackets are worked as stated after 2nd bracket.

Blanket

For the blanket, 48 square motifs are joined 6 wide x 8 deep, using join-as-you-go method: after completing first square, 7th round is used to join all subsequent squares. First, create a long strip of 8 squares where each square is joined along one side only, then begin to add the next strip, where first square is joined along one side, then all subsequent squares are joined along two sides (see 7th round). Once this strip is complete, add remaining strips in the same way.

Square motif

1st round (right side): With 4mm hook and Walnut, make a slip ring as follows; wind yarn round index finger of left hand to form a ring, insert hook into ring, yrh and pull through, 3ch (counts as 1tr here and throughout), 11tr into ring, ss in top of beginning 3ch to join – 12 tr.

2nd round: 3ch, 1tr in same st at base of beginning 3ch, 2tr in each st around, ss in top of beginning 3ch – 24 tr.

Fasten off. Turn to wrong side to work next 3 rounds.

3rd round: Join Gold with ss in any st, 1ch (does not count as a st here and throughout), starting in same st at base of beginning 1ch, [5tr-cl in next st, 2dc in next st] 12 times, ss in top of first 5tr-cl – 36 sts (made up of 12 5tr-cl and 24 dc).

Fasten off and keep wrong side facing.

4th round: Join Dandelion with ss in first st, 1ch, starting in same st at base of beginning 1ch, *5tr-cl in next st, 1dc in next st, [1dc, 5tr-cl] in next st, 1dc in each of next 2 sts, [5tr-cl, 1dc] in next st, 1dc in next st, 5tr-cl in next st, 2dc in next st; repeat from * a further 3 times, ss in top

of first 5tr-cl – 48 sts (made up of 16 5tr-cl and 32 dc). Fasten off and keep wrong side facing.

5th round: Join Citron with ss in first st, 1ch, starting in same st at base of beginning 1ch, *5tr-cl in next st, 1dc in each of next 2 sts, [5tr-cl, 1dc] in next st, 1dc in next st, 5tr-cl in next st, 1dc in next st, [1dc, 5tr-cl] in next st, 1dc in each of next 2 sts, 5tr-cl in next st, 2dc in next st; repeat from * a further 3 times, ss in top of first 5tr-cl – 60 sts (made up of 20 5tr-cl and 40 dc). Fasten off and turn work to right side to complete the square.

6th round (right side): Join Greengage with ss in any dc after a 5tr-cl, 3ch (counts as 1tr), 2tr in same st, [1ch, miss 2 sts, 3tr in next st] 3 times, miss 2 sts, [1ch, 3dtr, 2ch, 3dtr] in next st (for corner), *[miss 2 sts, 1ch, 3tr in next st] 4 times, miss 2 sts, [1ch, 3dtr, 2ch, 3dtr] in next st (for next corner); repeat from * twice more, 1ch, miss last 2 sts, ss in top of beginning 3ch – 4 3tr groups and 5 1ch-sps along each side and 4 corners of (3dtr, 2ch, 3dtr). Fasten off.

7th round (FOR FIRST SQUARE ONLY): Join White with ss in any ch-sp before a corner ch-sp, 3ch (counts as 1tr), 2tr in same ch-sp, *[1ch, 3tr, 2ch, 3tr] in corner ch-sp, [1ch, 3tr] in each ch-sp along side to next corner ch-sp; repeat from * to end of round, 1ch, ss in top of beginning 3ch and fasten off – 5 3tr groups and 6 1ch-sps along each side and 4 corners of (3tr, 2ch, 3tr).

7th round (FOR ALL SUBSEQUENT SQUARES):
As before, but when joining corners and side or sides as required, replace corner 2ch with '1ch, ss into corner of adjacent square' and replace 1ch along joining edge(s) with 'ss into the corresponding ch-sp of adjacent square where they meet'.
After working last square of blanket, continue with border.

Border

Stitch counts are not given as, depending on your tension, you may need to adjust your stitches to avoid your border being too loose or wavy.
To adjust stitches, work less stitches in the corners if needed, for example [1dc, 1ch, 1dc] in corner ch-sp.

1st round (right side): Join White with a ss in any corner ch-sp, 1ch (does not count as a st), *[1dc, 1ch, 1dc, 1ch, 1dc] in corner ch-sp, [1ch, skip 1 st, 1dc in next st or sp] to st before next corner of full blanket (and counting the joining sts of 7th round as 1 st), 1ch, skip 1 st; repeat from * around, ss in first dc, fasten off.

2nd round: Join Dandelion in any 1ch-sp along side of blanket, 1ch (does not count as a st), 1dc in same ch-sp, [1ch, skip 1 st, 1dc in next ch-sp] all around blanket, working [1dc, 1ch, 1dc, 1ch, 1dc] in each corner ch-sp, ss in first dc, fasten off.

3rd round: Join Walnut with a ss in any ch-sp, 1ch (does not count as a st), 2htr in each ch-sp around, working [2htr, 1ch, 2htr] in each corner ch-sp, ss in first htr, fasten off.
Weave in all ends and spray with cold water until damp, pin flat and leave to dry.

Cushion

Make 4 square motifs using same join-as-you-go method as for blanket, laid out 2 wide and 2 deep. With White, work 1st border round as for blanket, to neaten edges.
Take piece of fabric, fold each edge 1cm (approx ½in) to wrong side and iron flat to create a neat edge (and sew if preferred). Place fabric and cushion front with right sides together and sew around three edges using sewing needle and thread, then turn right side out. Insert cushion pad and sew final edge closed.

THE LAST ROUND OF EACH SQUARE IS WORKED USING A JOIN-AS-YOU-GO METHOD, SO THERE IS NO SEWING UP AT THE END

- [ ] EASY PEASY
- [x] A BIT MORE TRICKY
- [ ] HARD-ISH
- [ ] QUITE A CHALLENGE

South of the border blanket

Curl up under this beautiful blanket or use it as a decorative throw for your home!

Measurements

90 x 100cm (35½ x 39¼in).

Materials

You will need to use aran weight yarn in your chosen colour. Here we have used 14 x 50g (75m) balls of Drops Paris in Mustard (41).
4.5mm hook.
Yarn needle.

Tension

12 sts and 7 rows measure 9 x 9cm (3½ x 3½in) over treble crochet with a 4.5mm hook.

Note

At the beginning of a row, the ch 2 counts as first treble crochet. You will always work the last stitch of the following row into the top of this ch-2.

At the beginning of a row, the ch 3 counts as 1 tr and 1 ch. At the end of the following row, you will skip 1 st (this is the 1 ch) and work the last stitch into the top of the ch-2.

To make

Foundation row: Ch125, 1 tr in 4th ch from hook, 1tr in each st to end, turn. (123 sts)

Row 1: Ch 3, (counts as 1tr and 1ch), skip 1 st, *1 tr in next 19 sts, ch 1, skip 1 st**; rep from * to ** 5 times more, 1 tr in last st (in top of turning ch), turn.

Note: Each ch-sp also counts as 1 st, so when you reach a ch-sp you will work 1 tr into this, just as you would if it were a stitch (insert your hook into the space when you are working the stitch and not into the chain itself).

Row 2: Ch 2 (counts as 1tr), 1 tr in next 18 sts (working 1st tr into ch-sp from previous row), *ch 1, skip 1 st, 1 tr in next 3 sts, ch 1, skip 1 st, 1 tr in next 35 sts; rep from * once more, ch 1, skip 1 st, 1 tr in next 3 sts, ch 1, skip 1 st, 1 tr in next 19 sts, turn.

Row 3: Ch 3, skip 1 st, *1 tr in next 15 sts, ch 1, skip 1 st, 1 tr in next 7 sts, ch 1, skip 1 st, 1 tr in next 15 sts, ch 1, skip 1 st; rep from * twice more, 1 tr in last st, turn.

Row 4: Ch 2, 1 tr in next 14 sts, *ch 1, skip 1 st, 1 tr in next 5 sts, ch 1, skip 1 st, 1 tr in next 5 sts, ch 1, skip 1 st**, 1 tr in next 27 sts***; rep from * to *** once more then rep from * to ** once, 1 tr in next 15 sts, turn.

Row 5: Ch 3, skip 1 st, *1 tr in next 11 sts, ch 1, skip 1 st, 1 tr in next 5 sts, ch 1, skip 1 st, 1 tr in next 3 sts, ch 1, skip 1 st, 1 tr in next 5 sts, ch 1, skip 1 st, 1 tr in next 11 sts, ch 1, skip 1 st; rep from * twice more, 1 tr in last st, turn.

Row 6: Ch 2, 1 tr in next 10 sts, *ch 1, skip 1 st, 1 tr in next 5 sts, ch 1, skip 1 st, 1 tr in next 7 sts, ch 1, skip 1 st, 1 tr in next 5 sts, ch 1, skip 1 st**, 1 tr in next 19 sts***; rep from * to *** once more then rep from * to ** once, 1 tr in next 11 sts, turn.

Row 7: Ch 3, skip 1 st, *1 tr in next 13 sts, ch 1, skip 1 st, 1 tr in next 5 sts, ch 1, skip 1 st, 1 tr in next 5 sts, ch 1, skip 1 st, 1 tr in next 13 sts, ch 1, skip 1 st; rep from * twice more, 1 tr in last st, turn.

Row 8: Ch 2, 1 tr in next 12 sts, *ch 1, skip 1 st, 1 tr in next 5 sts, ch 1, skip 1 st, 1 tr in next 3 sts, ch 1, skip 1 st, 1 tr in next 5 sts, ch 1, skip 1 st**, 1 tr in next 23 sts***; rep from * to *** once more then rep from * to ** once, 1 tr in next 13 sts, turn.

Row 9: Ch 3, skip 1 st, *1 tr in next 9 sts, ch 1, skip 1 st, 1 tr in next 5 sts, ch 1, skip 1 st, 1 tr in next 7 sts, ch 1, skip 1 st, 1 tr in next 5 sts, ch 1, skip 1 st, 1 tr in next 9 sts, ch 1, skip 1 st; rep from * twice more, tr in last st, turn.

Row 10: Ch 2, 1 tr in next 14 sts, *ch 1, skip 1 st, 1 tr in next 5 sts, ch 1, skip 1 st, 1 tr in next 5 sts, ch 1, skip 1 st**, 1 tr in next 27 sts***; rep from * to *** once more then rep from * to ** once, 1 tr in next 15 sts, turn.

Row 11: Ch 3, skip 1 st, *1 tr in next 11 sts, ch 1, skip 1 st, 1 tr in next 5 sts, ch 1, skip 1 st, 1 tr in next 3 sts, ch 1, skip 1 st, 1 tr in next 5 sts, ch 1, skip 1 st, 1 tr in next 11 sts, ch 1, skip 1 st; rep from * twice more, 1 tr in last st, turn.

Row 12: Ch 2, 10 tr, *ch 1, skip 1 st, 1 tr in next 5 sts, ch 1, skip 1 st, 1 tr in next 3 sts, ch 1, skip 1 st, 1 tr in next 3 sts, ch 1, skip 1 st, 1 tr in next 5 sts, 1ch, skip 1 st**, 1 tr in next 19 sts***; rep from * to *** once more then rep from * to ** once, 1 tr in next 11 sts, turn.

Row 13: Ch 3, skip 1 st, *1 tr in next 13 sts, ch 1, skip 1 st, 1 tr in next 11 sts, ch 1, skip 1 st, 1 tr in next 13 sts, ch 1, skip 1 st; rep from * twice more, 1 tr in last st, turn.

Row 14: Ch 2, 1 tr in next 12 sts, *ch 1, skip 1 st, 1 tr in next 7 sts, ch 1, skip 1 st, 1 tr in next 7 sts, ch 1, skip 1 st**, 1 tr in next 23 sts***; rep from * to *** once more then rep from * to ** once, 1 tr in

next 13 sts, turn.
Row 15: Ch 3, skip 1 st, *1 tr in next 9 sts, ch 1, skip 1 st, 1 tr in next 19 sts, ch 1, skip 1 st, 1 tr in next 9 sts, ch 1, skip 1 st; rep from * twice more, 1 tr in last st, turn.
Row 16: Ch 2, 1 tr in next 2 sts, *ch 1, skip 1 st, 1 tr in next 17 sts, ch 1, skip 1 st, 1 tr in next 17 sts, ch 1, skip 1 st, 1 tr in next 3 sts; rep from * twice more, turn.
Row 17: Ch 2, 1 tr in next 4 sts, *ch 1, skip 1 st, 1 tr in next 31 sts, ch 1, skip 1 st, 1 tr in next 7 sts; rep from * once, ch 1, skip 1 st, 1 tr in next 31 sts, ch 1, skip 1 st, 1 tr in next 5 sts, turn.
Row 18: Ch 3, skip 1 st, *1 tr in next 5 sts, ch 1, skip 1 st, 1 tr in next 13 sts, ch 1, skip 1 st, 1 tr in next 13 sts, ch 1, skip 1 st, 1 tr in next 5 sts, ch 1, skip 1 st; rep from * twice more, tr in last st, turn.
Row 19: Ch 2, 1 tr in next 2 sts, *ch 1, skip 1 st, 1 tr in next 5 sts, ch 1, skip 1 st, 1 tr in next 23 sts, ch 1, skip 1 st, 1 tr in next 5 sts, ch 1, skip 1 st, 1 tr in next 3 sts; rep from * twice more, turn.
Row 20: Ch 2, 1 tr in next 4 sts, ch 1, skip 1 st, *1 tr in next 5 sts, ch 1, skip 1 st, 1 tr in next 9 sts, ch 1, skip 1 st, 1 tr in next 9 sts, ch 1, skip 1 st, 1 tr in next 5 sts**, ch 1, skip 1 st, 1 tr in next 7 sts, ch 1, skip 1 st***; rep from * to *** once more then rep from * to ** once, ch 1, skip 1 st, 1 tr in next 5 sts, turn.
Row 21: Ch 3, skip 1 st, *1 tr in next 5 sts, ch 1, skip 1 st, 1 tr in next 27 sts, ch 1, skip 1 st, 1 tr in next 5 sts, ch 1, skip 1 st; rep from * twice more, tr in last st, turn.
Row 22: Ch 2, 1 tr in next 2 sts, *ch 1, skip 1 st, 1 tr in next 5 sts, ch 1, skip 1 st, 1 tr in next 11 sts, ch 1, skip 1 st, 1 tr in next 11 sts, ch 1, skip 1 st, 1 tr in next 5 sts, ch 1, skip 1 st, 1 tr in next 3 sts; rep from * twice more, turn.
Row 23: Ch 2, 1 tr in next 4 sts, *ch 1, skip 1 st, 1 tr in next 5 sts, ch 1, skip 1 st, 1 tr in next 19 sts, ch 1, skip 1 st, 1 tr in next 5 sts, ch 1, skip 1 st**, 1 tr in next 7 sts***; rep from * to *** once more then rep from * to ** once, 1 tr in next 5 sts, turn.
Row 24: Ch 3, skip 1 st, *1 tr in next 5 sts, ch 1, skip 1 st, 1 tr in next 13 sts, ch 1, skip 1 st, 1 tr in next 13 sts, ch 1, skip 1 st, 1 tr in next 5 sts, ch 1, skip 1 st; rep from * twice more, 1 tr in last st, turn.
Row 25: Ch 2, 1 tr in next 2 sts, *ch 1, skip 1 st, 1 tr in next 5 sts, ch 1, skip 1 st, 1 tr in next 23 sts, ch 1, skip 1 st, 1 tr in

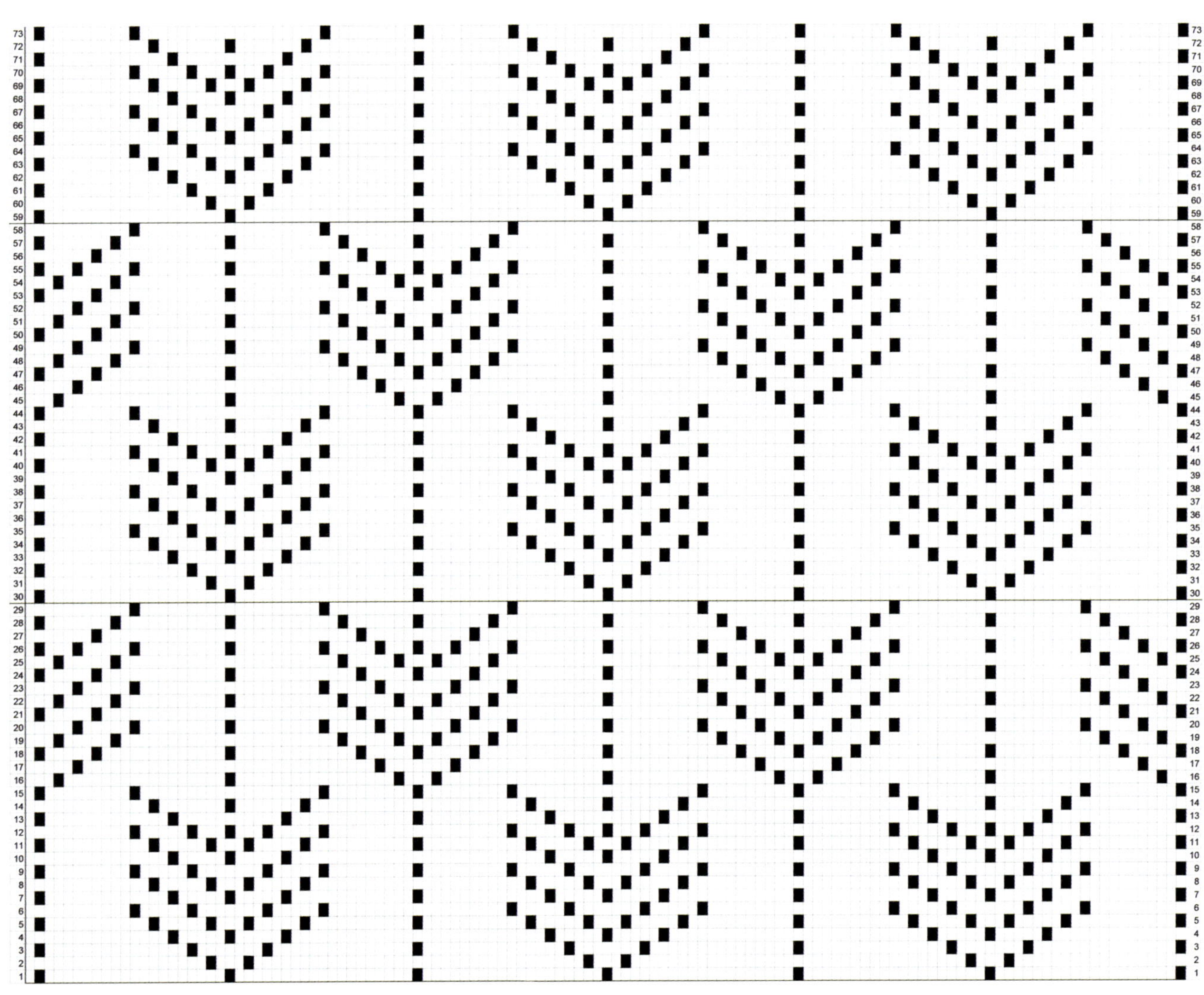

HTR 2 IN ROWS WHERE
THERE IS A SPACE
HTR 1 IN SOLID ROW ENDS

next 5 sts, ch 1, skip 1 st, 1 tr in next 3 sts; rep from * twice more, turn.
Row 26: Ch 3, *skip 1 st, 1 tr in next 3 sts, ch 1, skip 1 st, 1 tr in next 5 sts, ch 1, skip 1 st, 1 tr in next 9 sts, ch 1, skip 1 st, 1 tr in next 9 sts, ch 1, skip 1 st, 1 tr in next 5 sts, ch 1, skip 1 st, 1 tr in next 3 sts; rep from * twice more, ch 1, skip 1 st, 1 tr in last st, turn.
Row 27: Ch 2, 1 tr in next 6 sts, ch 1, skip 1 st, *1 tr in next 27 sts, ch 1, skip 1 st**, 1 tr in next 11 sts, ch 1, skip 1 st***; rep from * to *** once more then rep from * to ** once, 1 tr in next 7 sts, turn.
Row 28: Ch 3, skip 1 st, *1 tr in next 7 sts, ch 1, skip 1 st, 1 tr in next 11 sts, ch 1, skip 1 st, 1 tr in next 11 sts, ch 1, skip 1 st, 1 tr in next 7 sts, ch 1, skip 1 st; rep from * twice more, tr in last st, turn.
Row 29: Ch 2, 1 tr in next 10 sts, ch 1, skip 1 st, *1 tr in next 19 sts, ch 1, skip 1 st; rep from * 4 times, 1 tr in next 11 sts, turn.

ROWS 1-29 FORM THE PATTERN.
The pattern now repeats itself from row 1 to 29 and then from row 1 to 15. You should now have 74 rows (including the foundation row).

Row 75: Ch 2, 1 tr in each st and sp to the end, fasten off and weave in ends.

To give the blanket a neat finish you are now going to work a row of htrs along both sides of the blanket.
Start by joining the yarn in the bottom-right corner (around the post of the tr), ch 2 (counts as 1st htr), 1 htr in same space. Now work htrs all the way up the long side of the blanket by working 1 htr in solid row ends and 2 htr in rows where there is a space and finishing with 2 htr. Fasten off and weave in ends.

Repeat this process on the other side of the blanket by joining the yarn in the top-left corner and working down the second long side of blanket.

KATE ROWELL
Kate is a crochet designer based in the UK. She enjoys working with simple stitches and bright colours.
@jellybean_junction
blog.jellybeanjunction.co.uk

Granny square blankets

Use this versatile motif to create classic designs with a modern twist

✓ EASY PEASY
☐ A BIT MORE TRICKY
☐ HARD-ISH
☐ QUITE A CHALLENGE

Vintage style

This colourful project is perfect as a picnic blanket but equally lovely to snuggle up to indoors

To make

With 4mm hook and Fondant, make 4ch and ss in fourth ch from hook to form a ring. The blanket is worked in rounds, so for the first round you will be working your stitches into the ring; subsequent rounds will be worked into ch-sps and between the groups of 3tr.

1st round (right side): 3ch (counts as 1tr here and throughout), 2tr into the ring (this forms your first group of 3tr), [1ch, 3tr into the ring] 3 times, 1ch, ss in top of beginning 3ch – 4 groups of 3tr, 4 1ch-sps. Fasten off and turn work.

2nd round (wrong side): Join Lemon in any 1ch-sp, [3ch, 2tr, 1ch, 3tr] all into same 1ch-sp (to make first corner), [3tr, 1ch, 3tr] in each of next three 1ch-sps, ss in top of beginning 3ch – 24 tr and 4 1ch-sps. Fasten off and turn work.

3rd round: Join Pomegranate in any 1ch-sp, [3ch, 2tr, 1ch, 3tr] in same 1ch-sp, 3tr in each sp between the groups of 3tr along the side of your square to next corner 1ch-sp, *[3tr, 1ch, 3tr] in corner 1ch-sp, 3tr in each sp between the groups of 3tr along the side of your square to next corner; repeat from * twice more, ss in top of beginning 3ch – 9 tr and a 1ch-sp along each side. Fasten off and turn work.

3rd round sets the pattern. Continue in pattern using the following colour sequence, changing colour after each round and turning your work.

4th round: Join Meadow and work as 3rd round – 12 tr and a 1ch-sp along each side.

5th round: Join White and work as 3rd round – 15 tr and a 1ch-sp along each side.

6th round: Join Cloud Blue and work as 3rd round – 18 tr and a 1ch-sp along each side.

7th round: Join Parchment and work as 3rd round – 21 tr and a 1ch-sp along each side.

8th round: Join Shrimp and work as 3rd

Measurements

Complete blanket measures approximately 121 x 121cm (47¾ x 47¾ in).

Materials

For complete blanket: 1 x 100g (295m) ball of Stylecraft Special DK (100% acrylic) in each of Fondant (1241), Lemon (1020), Pomegranate (1083), Meadow (1065), White (1001), Cloud Blue (1019), Parchment (1218), Shrimp (1132), Denim (1302) and Cypress (1824).

Size 4mm crochet hook.

Tension

Tension is not critical for this pattern, although if you crochet very loose, you may need additional yarn than the amounts specified.

Abbreviations

Ch, chain; **st(s)**, stitch(es); **dc**, double crochet; **tr**, treble crochet; **htr**, half treble crochet; **ss**, slip stitch; **ch-sp(s)**, chain space(s); **yrh**, yarn round hook; **bobble st**, work a 4tr bobble stitch thus: *yrh, insert hook into st, yrh, pull up a loop, yrh, pull hook through first 2 loops on hook (leaving remaining loops on hook), repeat from * 3 times more (5 loops now remain on hook), yrh and pull through all loops on hook; **crab st**, work crab stitch thus: to start make 1ch, then insert your hook into the next stitch to the right, from the front to the back as normal, yrh, pull up a loop, yrh and pull through both loops on your hook (also known as reverse double crochet).

Note

The designer, Sue Rawlinson of Sweetpea Family Crochet, shares her handy tips for this design of blanket: "Crab stitch is the same as a regular dc, but the difference is that you are working in the opposite direction than you would usually work a dc. It can feel a little clumsy and awkward to start with but I'm sure it's worth it for the lovely twisted edging it gives you. To help your granny blanket remain flat and square, turn your work over after every round, you will start on a different side with each new colour. For this design, I stopped turning my work after 40th round, although it is important when working bobbles that you work on the wrong side of your blanket (this will be clearly noted in the pattern)."

Yarn amounts are based on average requirements and are therefore approximate. Instructions in square brackets are worked as stated after the 2nd bracket.

round – 24 tr and a 1ch-sp along each side.

9th round: Join Denim and work as 3rd round – 27 tr and a 1ch-sp along each side.

10th round: Join Cypress and work as 3rd round – 30 tr and a 1ch-sp along each side.

1st to 10th rounds form colour repeat pattern. Work another 3 full colour repeats, up to and including 40th round – 120 tr and a 1ch-sp along each side.

When working the following rounds, only turn work over when instructed.

41st round (wrong side): Join Fondant in any corner 1ch-sp, [2ch, 2htr, 1ch, 3htr] in same 1ch-sp, 1 bobble in centre tr of next group of 3tr, *[2htr in sp before next group of 3tr, 1 bobble in centre tr of next group of 3tr] to next corner 1ch-sp, [3htr, 1ch, 3htr] in corner 1ch-sp; repeat from * to end of round, ending last repeat before the corner, ss in top of beginning 2ch – 40 bobble sts, 84 htr and a 1ch-sp along each side. Turn work.

42nd round (right side): Join Lemon in any corner 1ch-sp, [3ch, 1tr, 1ch, 2tr] in same 1ch-sp, *[work 1tr in each htr and 1tr in each bobble st] to next corner 1ch-sp, [2tr, 1ch, 2tr] in corner 1ch-sp; repeat from * to end of round, ending last repeat before the corner, ss in top of beginning 3ch – 128 tr and a 1ch-sp along each side. Do not fasten off.

43rd round: Continuing with Lemon, 3ch (counts as first tr), work 1tr in each st and [2tr, 1ch, 2tr] in each corner 1ch-sp to end of round, ss in top of beginning 3ch – 132 tr and a 1ch-sp along each side. Fasten off.

44th round: Join Pomegranate in any corner 1ch-sp, [2ch, 1htr, 1ch, 2htr] in same 1ch-sp, work 1htr in each st and [2htr, 1ch, 2htr] in each corner 1ch-sp to end of round, ss in top of the beginning 2ch – 136 htr and a 1ch-sp along each side. Do not fasten off.

45th round: Continuing with Pomegranate, 2ch (counts as first htr), work 1htr in each st and [2htr, 1ch, 2htr] in each corner 1ch-sp to end of round, ss in top of beginning 2ch – 140 htr and a 1ch-sp along each side. Fasten off.

46th round: Join Meadow in any corner 1ch-sp and work as 44th round – 144 htr and a 1ch-sp along each side. Do not fasten off.

47th round: Continue with Meadow and work as 45th round – 148 htr and a

1ch-sp along each side.
48th round: Join White in any 1ch-sp, [1ch, 1dc, 1ch, 2dc] in same 1ch-sp, work 1dc in each st and [2dc, 1ch, 2dc] in each corner 1ch-sp to end of round, ss in top of beginning 1ch – 152 dc and a 1ch-sp along each side. Do not fasten off.
49th round: Continuing with White, 1ch (does not count as a st), 1dc in same st at base of 1ch, work 1dc in each st and [2dc, 1ch, 2dc] in each corner 1ch-sp to end of round, ss in top of first dc – 156 dc and a 1ch-sp along each side. Fasten off. Turn work over.
50th round (wrong side): Join Cloud Blue in any 1ch-sp, [2ch, 1htr, 1ch, 2htr] in same 1ch-sp, *1htr in next st, [1 bobble in next st, 1htr in each of next 2 sts] to last 2 sts before corner 1ch-sp, 1 bobble in next st, 1htr in next st, [2htr, 1ch, 2htr] in corner 1ch-sp; repeat from * to end of round, ending last repeat before corner, ss in top of beginning 2ch – 160 sts and a 1ch-sp along each side. Fasten off. Turn work over.
51st round (right side): Join Parchment in any 1ch-sp, [2ch, 1htr, 1ch, 2htr] in same 1ch-sp, work 1htr in each htr, 1htr in each bobble st and [2htr, 1ch, 2htr] in each corner st to end of round, ss in top of beginning 2ch – 164 sts and a 1ch-sp along each side. Fasten off.
52nd round: Join Shrimp in any corner 1ch-sp, [2ch, 1htr, 1ch, 2htr] in same 1ch-sp, work 1htr in each st and [2htr, 1ch, 2htr] in each corner 1ch-sp to end of round, ss in top of the beginning 2ch – 168 htr and a 1ch-sp along each side. Fasten off.
53rd round: Join Denim in any corner 1ch-sp and work as 52nd round – 172 htr and a 1ch-sp along each side. Fasten off.
54th round: Join Cypress in any 1ch-sp and work as 52nd round – 176 htr and a 1ch-sp along each side. Fasten off.
55th round: Join Pomegranate in any 1ch-sp and work as 52nd round – 180 htr and a 1ch-sp along each side. Fasten off.
56th round: Join Lemon in any 1ch-sp, [1ch, 1dc, 1ch, 2dc] in same 1ch-sp, work 1dc in each st and [2dc, 1ch, 2dc] in each corner 1ch-sp to end of round, ss in top of beginning 1ch – 184 dc and a 1ch-sp along each side.
Do not fasten off.
57th round: Continue with Lemon and ss into each st until you reach the corner 1ch-sp, work as 56th round – 188 dc and a 1ch-sp along each side.
Fasten off and turn work over.
58th round (wrong side): Join Fondant in any 1ch-sp, [2ch, 1htr, 1ch, 2htr] in same 1ch-sp, *1htr in each of next 3 sts, [1 bobble in next st, 1htr in each of next 4 sts] to next corner 1ch-sp, [2htr, 1ch, 2htr] in corner 1ch-sp; repeat from * to end of round, ending last repeat before corner, ss in top of beginning 2ch – 192 sts and a 1ch-sp along each side.
Note that on 58th round, if you find that your stitch count doesn't quite accommodate 4 htr in between each bobble don't worry, as this is a very forgiving repeat.
Fasten off and turn work over.
59th round (right side): Join Meadow in any 1ch-sp, [1ch, 1dc, 1ch, 2dc] in same 1ch-sp, work 1dc in each st and [2dc, 1ch, 2dc] in each corner 1ch-sp to end of round, ss in top of beginning 1ch – 196 dc and a 1ch-sp along each side. Do not fasten off.
60th round: Continue with Meadow and work 1dc in each st and [2dc, 1ch, 2dc] in each corner 1ch-sp, ss in top of beginning 1ch – 200 dc and a 1ch-sp along each side. Fasten off.
61st round: Join White in any 1ch-sp and work as 56th round – 204 dc and a 1ch-sp along each side. Fasten off.
62nd round: Join Cloud Blue in any 1ch-sp and work as 56th round – 208 dc and a 1ch-sp along each side. Fasten off.
63rd round: Join Parchment in any 1ch-sp and work as 56th round – 212 dc and a 1ch-sp along each side. Fasten off.
64th round: Join Shrimp in any 1ch-sp and work as 56th round – 216 dc and a 1ch-sp along each side. Fasten off.
65th round: Join Denim in any 1ch-sp and work as 56th round – 220 dc and a 1ch-sp along each side. Fasten off.
66th round: Join Cypress in any 1ch-sp and work as 56th round – 224 dc and a 1ch-sp along each side. Fasten off.
67th round: Join Pomegranate in any corner 1ch-sp, [2ch, 1htr, 1ch, 2htr] in same 1ch-sp, work 1htr in each st and [2htr, 1ch, 2htr] in each corner 1ch-sp to end of round, ss in top of the beginning 2ch – 228 htr and a 1ch-sp along each side. Fasten off.
68th round: Join Lemon into the first st after a corner. You will now work a crab stitch edging (see Abbreviations).
To start the round, make 1ch and insert your hook into the next stitch to the right, from the front to the back, pull up a loop, yrh and pull through both loops on your hook. Continue all around your blanket remembering to work [2 crab sts, 1ch, 2 crab sts] in each of the corner 1ch-sps, and when you reach the end of the round, ss in beginning 1ch and fasten off. Weave in your tail ends and you have finished your blanket.
Note that if you have difficulties with the crab stitch its well worth having a quick look on YouTube, you will find lots of easy to follow videos, but remember that this pattern uses UK terms.

Blanket band

With 4mm hook and any choice of colour, make 11ch.
1st row: 1dc in second ch from hook, 1dc

in each ch to end, turn – 10 sts.
2nd to 9th rows: 1ch (does not count as a st), 1dc in each st to end, turn.
10th row: 1ch (does not count as a st), 1dc in each st to end, changing to new colour of your choice on the last yrh of the last dc, turn.
Repeat 1st to 10th rows, 8 times more to work 90 rows in 9 different coloured stripes.
Do not change colour on last row.
91st row: Using the same colour yarn as 90th row, 1ch, work a ss into the first st of this row and also through the row-end st of the first row (you are joining the two ends of the strip together to form a circular band); continue to ss through both sets of sts to end. Fasten off and weave in tail ends.

Small strap

With 4mm hook and any choice of colour, make 6ch.
1st row: 1dc in second ch from hook, 1dc in each ch to end, turn – 5 sts.
2nd to 35th rows: 1ch (does not count as a st), 1dc in each st to end, turn. Fasten off.

Fold the small strap in half and sew onto your blanket band to form a decorative tab. For this blanket, it was attached onto the stripe crocheted in the same coloured yarn.

Flower

1st round: Using 4mm hook and Lemon, make a slip ring as follows: wind yarn round index finger of left hand to form a ring, insert hook into ring, yrh and pull through, 1ch, (does not count as a st) work 10dc in ring, ss in beginning 1ch, pull end of yarn tightly to close ring – 10 sts.
Fasten off.
2nd round: Join White into any st, starting in same st, work [3ch, 3tr, 3ch, ss] all in same st, *in next st work [3ch, 3tr, 3ch, ss]; repeat from * until you have 5 petals, ss in top of beginning 3ch.
Fasten off and weave in tail ends.
Finally, attach your flower onto the front of the band, just below the tab. Fold and roll up your blanket and slip it through the band, which will keep it perfectly in place.

Sweetpea blanket

In a beautiful spring palette, this blanket is worked in rows and is the perfect project for beginners

- ✓ EASY PEASY
- ☐ A BIT MORE TRICKY
- ☐ HARD-ISH
- ☐ QUITE A CHALLENGE

Measurements

Complete blanket measures approximately 89 x 132cm (35 x 52in), including border.

Materials

For complete blanket: 2 x 100g (295m) balls of Stylecraft Special DK (100% acrylic) in Cream (1005) and 1 ball in each of Cloud Blue (1019), Fondant (1241), Lincoln (1834), Lemon (1020), Sherbert (1034), Candyfloss (1130) and Spring Green (1316).
Size 5mm and 4mm crochet hooks; removable stitch markers (optional).

Tension

17 stitches and 10 rows, to 10 x 10cm (4 x 4in), over pattern, using 4mm hook.

Abbreviations

Ch, chain; **st(s)**, stitch(es); **dc**, double crochet; **tr**, treble crochet; **sp**, space; **yrh**, yarn round hook; **ss**, slip stitch.

Note

The starting chain is worked with a 5mm hook to prevent the first row from being too tight and to make the chains easier to work into. If you prefer, place a removable stitch marker in every 20th ch on your foundation chain, to help keep track of counting. On some rows, the last stitch of the row is the beginning 3ch from the previous row, which is always counted as a stitch. It is really important to finish with a tr in the top of this 3ch as this will keep your edges nice and straight and it will keep your stitch count correct. You may find it helpful to tick each numbered row off as you go along, especially if this is your first big project. Unless stated otherwise, when changing colours, break off the current yarn. Weave in yarn tails as you go along or at the end of each section. Yarn amounts are based on average requirements and are therefore approximate. Instructions in square brackets are worked as stated after 2nd bracket.

To make

Foundation chain: With 5mm hook and Cloud Blue, make 121ch.
Change to 4mm hook.

1st row: 1dc in 2nd ch from hook, [1dc in next ch] to end, turn – 120 sts.

2nd row: 1ch (does not count as a st throughout), [1dc in next st] to end, turn.

3rd row: 1ch, [1dc in next st] to end, turn.

4th row: As 3rd row, changing to Fondant on last yrh of last dc, turn.

5th row: 3ch (counts as 1tr throughout), skip st at base of 3ch, [1tr in next st] to end, turn.

6th row: 3ch, [1tr in next st] to end, changing to Cream on last yrh of last tr, turn.

7th and 8th rows: As 3rd and 4th rows, changing to Lincoln on last yrh of last dc of 8th row.

9th row: 1st Granny stripe row: 3ch, 1tr in st at base of 3ch, [skip 2 sts, 3tr in next st] to last 2 sts, skip 1 st, 1tr in last st, turn.

10th row: 2nd Granny stripe row: 3ch, 1tr in st at base of 3ch, [3tr in sp between next 2 tr-groups] to last 2 sts, skip 1 st, 1tr in last st, turn.

11th row: 3rd Granny stripe row: As 10th row, changing to Cream on last yrh of last tr, turn.

12th and 13th rows: As 3rd and 4th rows, changing to Lemon on last yrh of last dc of 13th row, turn.

14th and 15th rows: As 9th and 10th rows.

16th and 17th rows: As 10th and 11th rows, changing to Cream on last yrh of last tr of 17th row, turn.

18th and 19th rows: As 3rd and 4th rows, changing to Sherbert on last yrh of last dc of 19th row, turn.

20th and 21st rows: As 5th and 6th rows, changing to Candyfloss on last yrh of last tr of 21st row, turn.

22nd and 23th rows: As 5th and 6th rows, changing to Cream on last yrh of last tr of 23rd row, turn.

24th and 25th rows: As 3rd and 4th rows, changing to Spring Green on last yrh of last dc of 25th row, turn.

26th and 27th rows: As 9th and 10th rows.

28th and 29th rows: As 10th and 11th rows, changing to Cream on last yrh of last tr of 29th row, turn.

30th and 31st rows: As 3rd and 4th rows, changing to Cloud Blue on last yrh of last dc of 31st row, turn.

32th to 34th rows: As 9th to 11th rows, changing to Cream on last yrh of last tr of 34th row, turn.

35th and 36th rows: As 3rd and 4th rows, changing to Fondant on last yrh of last dc of 36th row, turn.

37th and 38th rows: As 5th and 6th rows, changing to Lincoln on last yrh of last tr of 38th row, turn.

39th and 40th rows: As 5th and 6th rows, changing to Cream on last yrh of last tr of 40th row, turn.

41st row: 1ch, [1dc in next st] to end, turn.

42nd row: As 41st row, changing to Lemon on last yrh of last dc, turn.

43rd row: 1st V-stitch row: 3ch, skip st at base of 3ch, 2tr in next st, [skip next st, 2tr in next st] to last 2 sts, skip next st, 1tr in last st, changing to Sherbert on last yrh of last tr, turn.

44th row: 2nd V-stitch row: 3ch, [2tr in sp between the 2 tr of next 2tr-gp] to last st, 1tr in last st, changing to Candyfloss on last yrh of last tr, turn.

45th row: 3rd V-stitch row: As 44th row, changing to Spring Green on last yrh of last tr, turn.

46th row: 4th V-stitch row: As 44th row, changing to Cream on last yrh of last tr, turn.

47th and 48th rows: As 41st and 42nd rows, changing to Cloud Blue on last yrh of last dc of 48th row, turn.

49th row: As 43rd row, changing to Fondant on last yrh of last tr, turn.

50th row: As 44th row, changing to Lincoln on last yrh of last tr, turn.

51st row: As 44th row, changing to Cream on last yrh of last tr, turn.

52nd and 53rd rows: As 41st and 42nd rows, changing to Lemon on last yrh of last dc of 53rd row, turn.

54th row: 3ch, skip st at base of 3ch, [1tr in next st] to end, turn.

55th row: As 54th row, changing to Sherbert on last yrh of last tr, turn.

56th and 57th rows: As 54th and 55th rows, changing to Cream on last yrh of last tr of 57th row, turn.

58th and 59th rows: As 41st and 42nd rows, changing to Candyfloss on last yrh of last dc of 59th row, turn.

60th row: As 43rd row, changing to Spring Green on last yrh of last tr, turn.

61st row: As 44th row, changing to Cloud

Blue on last yrh of last tr, turn.
62nd row: As 44th row, changing to Fondant on last yrh of last tr, turn.
63rd row: As 44th row, changing to Cream on last yrh of last tr, turn.
64th and 65th rows: As 41st and 42nd rows, changing to Lincoln on last yrh of last dc of 65th row, turn.
66th row: As 43rd row, changing to Lemon on last yrh of last tr, turn.
67th row: As 44th row, changing to Sherbert on last yrh of last tr, turn.
68th row: As 44th row, changing to Cream on last yrh of last tr, turn.
69th and 70th rows: As 41st and 42nd rows, changing to Candyfloss on last yrh of last dc of 70th row, turn.
71st and 72nd rows: As 54th and 55th rows, changing to Spring Green on last yrh of last tr of 72nd row, turn.
73rd and 74th rows: As 54th and 55th rows, changing to Cream on last yrh of last tr of 74th row, turn.
75th and 76th rows: As 41st and 42nd rows, but changing to Cloud Blue on last yrh of last dc of 76th row, turn.
77th row: 1st Granny stripe row: 3ch, 1tr in st at base of 3ch, [skip 2 sts, 3tr in next st] to last 2 sts, skip 1 st, 1tr in last st, turn.
78th row: 2nd Granny stripe row: 3ch, 1tr in st at base of 3ch, [3tr in sp between next 2 tr-groups] to last 2 sts, skip 1 st, 1tr in last st, turn.
79th row: 3rd Granny stripe row: As 78th row, changing to Cream on last yrh of last tr, turn.
80th row: 1ch, [1dc in next st] to end, turn.
81st row: As 80th row, changing to Fondant on last yrh of last dc, turn.
82nd and 83rd rows: As 77th and 78th rows.
84th and 85th rows: As 78th and 79th rows, changing to Cream on last yrh of last tr of 85th row, turn.
86th and 87th rows: As 80th and 81st rows, changing to Lincoln on last yrh of last dc of 87th row, turn.
88th row: 3ch, skip st at base of 3ch, [1tr in next st] to end, turn.
89th row: As 88th row, changing to Lemon on last yrh of last tr, turn.
90th and 91st rows: As 88th and 89th rows, changing to Cream on last yrh of last tr of 91st row, turn.
92nd and 93rd rows: As 80th and 81st rows, changing to Sherbert on last yrh of last dc of 93rd row, turn.
94th and 95th rows: As 77th and 78th rows.

96th and 97th rows: As 78th and 79th rows, changing to Cream on last yrh of last tr of 97th row, turn.
98th and 99th rows: As 80th and 81st rows, changing to Candyfloss on last yrh of last dc of 99th row, turn.
100th to 102nd rows: As 77th to 79th rows, and change to Cream on last yrh of last tr of 102nd row, turn.
103rd and 104th rows: As 80th and 81st rows, changing to Spring Green on last yrh of last dc of 104th row, turn.
105th and 106th rows: As 88th and 89th rows, changing to Cloud Blue on last yrh of last tr of 106th row, turn.
107th and 108th rows: As 88th and 89th rows, changing to Cream on last yrh of last tr of 108th row, turn.
109th row: 1ch, [1dc in next st] to end, turn.
110th row: As 109th row, changing to Fondant on last yrh of last dc, turn.
111th row: 1st V-stitch row: 3ch, skip st at base of 3ch, 2tr in next st, [skip next st, 2tr in next st] to last 2 sts, skip next st, 1tr in last st, changing to Lincoln on last yrh of last tr, turn.
112th row: 2nd V-stitch row: 3ch, [2tr in sp between the 2 tr of next 2tr-gp] to last st, 1tr in last st, changing to Lemon on last yrh of last tr, turn.
113th row: 3rd V-stitch row: As 112th row, changing to Sherbert on last yrh of last tr, turn.
114th row: 4th V-stitch row: As 112th row, changing to Cream on last yrh of last tr, turn.
115th and 116th rows: As 109th and 110th rows, changing to Candyfloss on last yrh of last dc of 116th row, turn.
117th row: As 111th row, changing to Spring Green on last yrh of last tr, turn.
118th row: As 112th row, changing to Cloud Blue on last yrh of last tr, turn.
119th row: As 112th row, changing to Cream on last yrh of last tr, turn.
120th and 121st rows: As 109th and 110th rows, changing to Fondant on last yrh of last dc of 121st row, turn.
122nd row: 3ch, skip st at base of 3ch, [1tr in next st] to end, turn.
123rd row: As 122nd row, changing to Lincoln on last yrh of last tr, turn.
124th and 125th rows: As 122nd and 123rd rows, changing to Cream on last yrh of last tr of 125th row, turn.
126th and 127th rows: As 109th and 110th rows, changing to Lemon on last yrh of last dc of 127th row, turn.
128th row: As 111th row, changing to Sherbert on last yrh of last tr, turn.
129th row: As 112th row, changing to Candyfloss on last yrh of last tr, turn.
130th row: As 112th row, changing to Spring Green on last yrh of last tr, turn.
131st row: As 112th row, changing to Cream on last yrh of last tr, turn
132nd and 133rd rows: As 109th and 110th rows, changing to Cloud Blue on last yrh of last dc of 110th row, turn.
134th row: As 111th row, changing to Fondant on last yrh of last tr, turn.
135th row: As 112th row, changing to Lincoln on last yrh of last tr, turn.
136th row: As 112th row, changing to Cream on last yrh of last tr, turn.
137th and 138th rows: As 109th and 110th rows, changing to Lemon on last yrh of last dc of 138th row, turn.
139th row: As 122nd row, changing to Sherbert on last yrh of last tr, turn.
140th to 143rd rows: As 109th row. Fasten off.

Note

When working the border, especially along the row-ends, work a section at a time and check your tension. If your work is pulling, add a few more trebles evenly spaced; if the work is wavy and loose, decrease the number of trebles along the sides evenly spaced.

Unless stated otherwise, when changing colours, break off the current yarn. To avoid a daunting task, weave in yarn tails as you go along.

With 4mm hook and Cream, hold blanket with Cloud Blue foundation ch uppermost and join yarn with ss to right-hand corner. Work along opposite loops of foundation chain and work in rounds that are joined.

1st round: 3ch (counts as 1tr throughout), *[1tr in next st] to next corner, work 3tr in corner st, [1tr in each dc row-end and 2tr in each tr row-end] to next corner, work 3tr in corner st; repeat from * once more, ss in beginning 3ch.
2nd round: 1ch (does not count as a st throughout), *[1dc in next st] to next corner, work 3dc in corner st; repeat from * to end, ss in beginning 1ch.
3rd round: Join Lincoln to st to left of top-right corner st. As 2nd round.
4th round: Join Lemon to st to left of top-right corner st. As 2nd round.
5th round: Join Sherbert to st to left of top-right corner st. As 2nd round.
6th round: Join Candyfloss to st to left of top-right corner st. As 2nd round.
7th round: Join Cream to st to left of top-right corner st. As 2nd round.
8th round: With Cream, 3ch, * 1tr in next st] to next corner, 3tr in corner st; repeat from * to end, ss in beginning 3ch.
9th round: Join Spring Green to any st, 1ch, [ss in next st] to end. Fasten off.
Edging round: With wrong side facing, join Cream and work along back of blanket, 3ch (not counted as a st), 1tr in same st at base of beginning 3ch, [ss in next st, 1tr in next st] to end, ss into top of first tr. Fasten off. Neaten your final tails and you are finished. Enjoy snuggling with your beautiful blanket!

☐ EASY PEASY
☑ A BIT MORE TRICKY
☐ HARD-ISH
☐ QUITE A CHALLENGE

Flower garden blanket

Designed by Lynne Rowe with an exclusive colourway by Heather Leal for The Knitting Network

Measurements

Each square measures approx 13 x 13cm (5 x 5in). When complete, the blanket will measure approximately 108 x 108cm (42½ x 42½in), including edging.

Materials

For complete blanket: 4 x 100g (196m) balls of Stylecraft Special Aran (100% acrylic) in Cream (1005); 1 ball in each of Pomegranate (1083), Lipstick (1246), Fondant (1241), Spice (1711) Magenta (1084), Plum (1061), Lemon (1020) and Meadow (1065).
Size 5mm crochet hook.

Abbreviations

Ch, chain; **dc**, double crochet; **st**, stitch; **htr**, half treble; **tr**, treble; **dc2tog**, double crochet 2 together; **htr2tog**, half treble crochet 2 together; **ss**, slip st; **ch-sp**, chain space; **chlp**, chain loop; **yrh**, yarn round hook.

Note

Yarn amounts are based on average requirements and are therefore approximate. Instructions in square brackets are worked as stated after 2nd bracket. The entire blanket will require 4 daisy squares, 12 circle centre squares and 20 sunburst granny squares.

Daisy square

First square

With 5mm hook and Fondant, make 5ch, ss in first ch to form ring.

1st round: 3ch (counts as 1tr), 3tr into ring, turn, 3ch, 1tr in base of 3ch, 1tr in each of next 2tr, 1tr in top of 3ch – petal made, turn, [3ch, take this ch across back of petal just made, 4tr into ring, turn, 3ch, 1tr in base of 3ch, 1tr in each of next 3tr – petal made, turn] 7 times, 3ch, ss in 3rd of 3ch at beginning of 1st round – 8 petals. Fasten off.

2nd round: Join Pomegranate with a ss to chlp behind any petal, 3ch (counts as 1tr), work 2tr, 2ch and 3tr around same chlp as join, [3tr around chlp behind next petal, work 3tr, 2ch and 3tr around chlp behind next petal] 3 times, 3tr around last chlp, ss in 3rd of 3ch.

3rd round: Ss into each of next 2tr, ss in corner ch-sp, 3ch (counts as 1tr), work 2tr, 2ch and 3tr in same corner ch-sp, [miss next tr, 1tr in each of next 7tr, miss next tr, work 3tr, 2ch and 3tr in next corner ch-sp] 3 times, miss next tr, 1tr in each of next 7tr, miss next tr, ss in 3rd of 3ch. Fasten off.

4th round: Join Cream with a ss to any corner ch-sp, 3ch (counts as 1tr), work 2tr, 2ch and 3tr in same ch-sp as join, *1tr in each of next 3tr, [1ch, miss next tr, 1tr in next tr] 3 times, 1ch, miss next tr, 1tr in each of next 3tr, work 3tr, 2ch and 3tr in corner ch-sp, repeat from * twice more, 1tr in each of next 3tr, [1ch, miss next tr, 1tr in next tr] 3 times, 1ch, miss next tr, 1tr in each of last 3tr, ss in 3rd of 3ch. Fasten off.

Second square

Using Magenta instead of Fondant and Plum instead of Pomegranate, work as first square.

Third square

Using Spice instead of Fondant and

THE SECOND SQUARE

Lipstick instead of Pomegranate, work as first square.

Fourth square
Using Lemon instead of Fondant and Meadow instead of Pomegranate, work as first square.

Circle in a square

First square (make 3)
With 5mm hook and Magenta, make 4ch, ss into first ch to form a ring.
1st round: 3ch (counts as 1tr), 15tr into ring, ss in 3rd of 3ch.
2nd round: 3ch (counts as 1tr), 1tr in base of 3ch, 2tr in each tr to end, ss in 3rd of 3ch – 32 sts. Fasten off.
3rd round: Join Plum with a ss to any tr, 3ch (counts as 1tr), 1tr in base of 3ch, 1tr in next tr, [2tr in next tr, 1tr in next tr] to end, ss in 3rd of 3ch – 48 sts.
4th round: 2ch (counts as 1htr), miss next 2tr, [work 3tr, 2ch and 3tr in next tr, miss next 2tr, 1htr in each of next 2tr, 1dc into each of next 3tr, 1htr in each of next 2tr, miss next 2tr] 3 times, work 3tr, 2ch and 3tr in next tr, miss next 2tr, 1htr in each of next 2tr, 1dc into each of next 3tr, 1htr in last tr, ss in 2nd of 2ch.
Fasten off.
5th round: Join Cream with a ss to any corner ch-sp, 3ch (counts as 1tr), work 2tr, 2ch and 3tr in same ch-sp as join, *1tr in each of next 3tr, [1ch, miss next st, 1tr in next st] 3 times, 1ch, miss next st, 1tr in each of next 3tr, work 3tr, 2ch and 3tr in corner ch-sp, repeat from * twice more, 1tr in each of next 3tr, [1ch, miss next st, 1tr in next st] 3 times, 1ch, miss next st, 1tr in each of last 3tr, ss in 3rd of 3ch.
Fasten off.

Second square (make 3)
Using Fondant instead of Magenta and Pomegranate instead of Plum, work as first square.

Third square (make 3) Using Spice instead of Magenta and Lipstick instead of Plum, work as first square.

Fourth square (make 3) Using Lemon instead of Magenta and Meadow instead of Plum, work as first square.

GORGEOUS CLUSTER STITCHES CREATE THIS THIRD SQUARE

Sunburst granny square

First square (make 5)

With 5mm hook and Meadow, make 4ch, ss in first ch to form ring.

1st round: 3ch (counts as 1tr), 15tr into ring, ss in 3rd of 3ch.

2nd round: Yrh, insert hook in same place as ss, yrh and pull through, [yrh, insert hook in same st, yrh and pull through] twice, yrh and pull through all 7 loops on hook – puff st made, 1ch, [puff st into next st, 1ch] 15 times, ss in top of first puff st – 16 puff sts. Fasten off.

3rd round: Join Lemon with a ss to any ch-sp, 2ch, [yrh, insert hook in same ch-sp as join, yrh and pull through, yrh and pull through first 2 loops on hook] twice, yrh and pull through all 3 loops on hook – 2-st cluster made, 2ch, *yrh, insert hook in next ch-sp, yrh and pull through, yrh and pull through first 2 loops on hook, [yrh, insert hook in same ch-sp, yrh and pull through, yrh and pull through first 2 loops on hook] twice, yrh and pull through all 4 loops on hook – 3-st cluster made, 2ch, repeat from * to end, ss in top of first cluster. Fasten off.

4th round: Join Meadow with a ss to any ch-sp, 2ch (counts as 1htr), 1htr in same ch-sp as join, miss next cluster, [work 3tr, 2ch and 3tr in next ch-sp, miss next cluster, 1htr in next ch-sp, 1htr in top of next cluster, 2dc in next ch-sp, 1dc in top of next cluster, 2htr in next ch-sp, miss next cluster] 3 times, work 3tr, 2ch and 3tr in next ch-sp, miss next cluster, 1htr in next ch-sp, 1htr in top of next cluster, 2dc in next ch-sp, 1dc in top of next cluster, ss in 2nd of 2ch. Fasten off.

5th round: Join Cream with a ss to any corner ch-sp, 3ch (counts as 1tr), work 2tr, 2ch and 3tr in same ch-sp as join, *1tr in each of next 3tr, [1ch, miss next st, 1tr in next st] 3 times, 1ch, miss next st, 1tr in each of next 3tr, work 3tr, 2ch and 3tr in corner ch-sp, repeat from * twice more, 1tr in each of next 3tr, [1ch, miss next st, 1tr in next st] 3 times, 1ch, miss next st, 1tr in each of last 3tr, ss in 3rd of 3ch. Fasten off.

Second square (make 5)

Using Plum instead of Meadow and Magenta instead of Lemon, work as first square.

Third square (make 5)

Using Lipstick instead of Meadow and Spice instead of Lemon, work as first square.

Fourth square (make 5)

Using Pomegranate instead of Meadow and Fondant instead of Lemon, work as first square.

Border

Beginning each time at top-left corner and working clockwise arrange squares as follows:

Place 4 daisy squares to form large square for middle of blanket in following daisy colour order: Spice, Lemon, Fondant and Magenta. Surround the first 4 squares by circle in square squares with following centres: 1 Spice, 2 Magenta, 1 Lemon, 2 Spice, 1 Fondant, 2 Lemon, 1 Magenta and 2 Fondant. Place sunburst granny squares around previous squares with centres in following colours: 1 Lipstick, 1 Meadow, 2 Pomegranate, 1 Lipstick, 1 Meadow, 1 Pomegranate, 2 Plum, 1 Meadow, 1 Pomegranate, 1 Plum, 2 Lipstick, 1 Pomegrante, 1 Plum, 1 Lipstick, 2 Meadow and 1 Plum.

Working horizontally and with wrong sides together, join squares using 5mm hook and Cream, by working 1dc into the back loops of each corresponding pair of stitches.
Join squares vertically in same way.

Border

With right side facing and using 5mm hook, join Cream with ss to any corner ch-sp.

1st round: Work 2dc, 1ch and 2dc in same ch-sp as join, **miss next tr, 1dc in each of next 5tr, [1dc in next ch-sp, 1dc in next tr] 3 times, 1dc in next ch-sp, 1dc in each of next 5tr, *dc2tog over next tr and in ch-sp, 1dc in joining seam, dc2tog in next ch-sp and next tr, 1dc in each of next 5tr, [1dc in next ch-sp, 1dc in next tr] 3 times, 1dc in next ch-sp, 1dc in each of next 5tr, repeat from * 4 times more ***, miss 1tr, work 2dc, 1ch and 2dc in corner ch-sp, repeat from ** twice more, then work from ** to ***, miss 1tr, ss in first dc – 121dc along each side.

2nd round: Ss along and into first ch-sp, 2ch (counts as 1htr), work 1htr, 2ch and 2htr in same ch-sp as last ss, *miss next dc, [1htr in each of next 18dc, htr2tog] 5 times, 1htr in each of next 19dc, miss 1dc **, work 2htr, 2ch and 2htr in next ch-sp, repeat from * twice more, then work from

* to **, ss in 2nd of 2ch – 118htr along each side. Fasten off.
Join Lipstick with ss to any corner ch-sp.
3rd round: 3ch (counts as 1tr), work 1tr, 2ch and 2tr in same ch-sp as ss, *miss 1htr, 1tr in each htr to next corner ch-sp, work 2tr, 2ch and 2tr in next ch-sp, repeat from * twice more, miss 1htr, 1tr in each htr to end, ss in 3rd of 3ch – 121tr along each side. Fasten off.
Join Cream with ss to any corner ch-sp.
4th round: 3ch (counts as 1tr), work 1tr, 2ch and 2tr in same ch-sp as ss, *1tr in each of next 30tr, [1ch, miss 1tr, 1tr in next tr] 30 times, 1ch, miss 1tr, 1tr in each of next 30tr **, work 2tr, 2ch and 2tr in next ch-sp, repeat from * twice more, then work from * to **, ss in 3rd of 3ch. Fasten off.
Join Meadow with ss to any corner ch-sp.
5th round: 3ch (counts as 1tr), work 1tr, 2ch and 2tr in same ch-sp as ss, *1tr in each of next 32tr, [1tr in next ch-sp, 1tr in next tr] 30 times, 1tr in next ch-sp, 1tr in each of next 32tr **, work 2tr, 2ch and 2tr in next ch-sp, repeat from * twice more, then work from * to **, ss in 3rd of 3ch – 129tr along each side. Fasten off. Join Fondant with ss to any corner ch-sp.
6th round: 3ch (counts as 1tr), work 1tr, 2ch and 2tr in same ch-sp as ss, *1tr in each tr to corner ch-sp, work 2tr, 2ch and 2tr in corner ch-sp, repeat from * twice more, 1tr in each tr to end, ss in 3rd of 3ch – 133tr along each side. Fasten off. Join Spice with ss to any corner ch-sp.
7th round: As 6th round – 137tr along each side. Fasten off. Join Cream with ss to any corner ch-sp.
8th round: 3ch (counts as 1tr), work 1tr, 2ch and 2tr in same ch-sp as ss, *miss 1tr, 1tr in each of next 37tr, [1ch, miss 1tr, 1tr in next tr] 30 times, 1ch, miss 1tr, 1tr in each of next 37tr, miss 1tr **, work 2tr, 2ch and 2tr in next ch-sp, repeat from * twice more, then work from * to **, ss in 3rd of 3ch. Fasten off. Join Magenta with ss to any corner ch-sp.
9th round: 3ch (counts as 1tr), work 1tr, 2ch and 2tr in same ch-sp as ss, *1tr in each of next 39tr, [1tr in next ch-sp, 1tr in next tr] 30 times, 1ch, miss 1tr, 1tr in each of next 39tr **, work 2tr, 2ch and 2tr in next ch-sp, repeat from * twice more, then work from * to **, ss in 3rd of 3ch – 143tr along each side. Fasten off. Join Cream with ss to any corner ch-sp.
10th round: 1dc in same ch-sp as ss, *[5ch, miss next 3tr, 1dc in next tr] to corner ch-sp, 5ch, 1dc in corner ch-sp, repeat from * twice more, [5ch, miss next 3tr, 1dc in next tr] end, ending last repeat with ss in first dc.
11th round: Work 1dc, 3tr and 1dc in each ch-sp to end, ss in first dc.
Fasten off and neaten ends.

Granny square throw

Create this wonderfully colourful, shabby chic throw using a large motif in a mix of colours

- ☐ EASY PEASY
- ☑ A BIT MORE TRICKY
- ☐ HARD-ISH
- ☐ QUITE A CHALLENGE

Measurements

The completed throw measures approximately 117 x 145cm (46 x 57in), including edging.

Materials

Bergere de France Ideal (40% wool, 30% acrylic, 30% polyamide) in 50g (125m) balls. Entire blanket requires the following:

Key colours: 3 balls in each of Meije (51253), Olivine (20754) and Vannerie (23316).
2 balls in each of Cyclamen (20555) and Danseuse (23026).

Other colours: 2 balls in each of Linaire (20933), Lievre (54695) and Beige Rose (35177).
1 ball in each of Myosotis (20841), Jaune (35166), Pinede (25324), Belladone (22375), Vitamine (24109), Cendre (24241), Persan (24257) and Sequoia (35168).

Joining and edging: 5 balls Everest (51220).
Size 4mm crochet hook.

Tension

Large motif measures approx. 24 x 24cm (9.4 x 9.4in), medium motif measures approx. 12 x 12cm (4.7 x 4.7in) and small motif measures approx. 6 x 6cm (2.3 x 2.3in); using 4mm hook.

Abbreviations

Ch, chain; **ch-sp**, chain space; **dc**, double crochet, **htr**, half treble; **tr**, treble; **sp**, space; **st**, stitch; **ss**, slip stitch; **yrh**, yarn over hook; **tr2tog**, work 2tr together thus: [yrh, insert hook in ch-sp indicated, yrh and pull through, yrh and pull through first 2 loops on hook] twice, yrh and pull through all 3 loops on hook; **tr3tog**, work 3tr together thus: [yrh, insert hook in ch-sp indicated, yrh and pull through, yrh and pull through first 2 loops on hook] 3 times.

Note

Yarn amounts are approximate. Instructions in square brackets are worked as stated after 2nd bracket.

Square one

Large motif

(Make 6)

Use 3 or more colours, varying the number of colours on each square and include at least one of the key colours. Work all even-numbered rounds in the same colour – colour Z.

1st round: With 4.00 hook and chosen colour, make 4ch, 2tr in 4th ch from hook, 3ch, [3tr, 3ch] 3times in same place first 2tr, ss in 3rd of 3ch. Fasten off.

2nd round: Join Z to any 3-ch-sp of last round, 1ch, [1dc, 3ch] twice in same place as join, *[1dc, 3ch] twice in next 3-ch-sp, repeat from * twice more, ss in first dc. Fasten off.

3rd round: Join next colour in last 3-ch-sp of last round, 3ch (counts as 1tr throughout), 2tr in same place as join, [work 3tr, 3ch and 3tr in corner 3-ch-sp, 3tr in next 3-ch-sp] 3 times, work 3tr, 3ch and 3tr in last corner 3-ch-sp, ss in 3rd of 3ch. Fasten off.

4th round: Join Z in sp between 3-tr group at end and 3ch at start of last round,1ch, 1dc in same place as join, 3ch, 1dc in next sp between 3-tr groups, 3ch, *[1dc, 3ch] twice in corner 3-ch-sp, [1dc in next sp between 3-tr groups, 3ch] twice, repeat from * twice more, [1dc, 3ch] twice in corner 3-ch-sp, ss in first dc. Fasten off.

5th round: Join next colour in last 3-ch-sp of last round, 3ch, 2tr in same place as join, [3tr in each 3-ch-sp to corner, work 3tr, 3ch and 3tr in corner 3-ch-sp] 4 times, ss in 3rd of 3ch. Fasten off.

6th round: Join Z in sp between 3-tr group at end and 3ch at start of last round, 1ch, 1dc in same place as join, 3ch, *[1dc in next sp between 3-tr groups, 3ch] to corner, [1dc, 3ch] twice in corner 3-ch-sp, repeat from * 3 times, ss in first dc. Fasten off.

7th to 16th rounds: Repeat 5th and 6th rounds 5 times. Fasten off.

17th round: Join next colour in last 3-ch-sp of last round, 2ch, 2dc in same place as join, [3dc in each 3-ch-sp to corner, work 3dc, 1ch and 3dc in corner 3-ch-sp] 4 times, ss in 2nd of 2ch. Fasten off.

TREBLES, DCS AND CHAIN ARE WORKED HERE TO CREATE A NEAT NEW LOOK

Measurements

The completed throw measures approximately 117 x 145cm (46 x 57in), including edging.

Materials

Bergere de France Ideal (40% wool, 30% acrylic, 30% polyamide) in 50g (125m) balls. Entire blanket requires the following:
Key colours: 3 balls in each of Meije (51253), Olivine (20754) and Vannerie (23316).
2 balls in each of Cyclamen (20555) and Danseuse (23026).
Other colours: 2 balls in each of Linaire (20933), Lievre (54695) and Beige Rose (35177).
1 ball in each of Myosotis (20841), Jaune (35166), Pinede (25324), Belladone (22375), Vitamine (24109), Cendre (24241), Persan (24257) and Sequoia (35168).
Joining and edging: 5 balls Everest (51220).
Size 4mm crochet hook.

Tension

Large motif measures approx. 24 x 24cm (9.4 x 9.4in), medium motif measures approx. 12 x 12cm (4.7 x 4.7in) and small motif measures approx. 6 x 6cm (2.3 x 2.3in); using 4mm hook.

Abbreviations

Ch, chain; **ch-sp**, chain space; **dc**, double crochet; **htr**, half treble; **tr**, treble; **sp**, space; **st**, stitch; **ss**, slip stitch; **yrh**, yarn over hook; **tr2tog**, work 2tr together thus: [yrh, insert hook in ch-sp indicated, yrh and pull through, yrh and pull through first 2 loops on hook] twice, yrh and pull through all 3 loops on hook; **tr3tog**, work 3tr together thus: [yrh, insert hook in ch-sp indicated, yrh and pull through, yrh and pull through first 2 loops on hook] 3 times.

Note

Yarn amounts are approximate. Instructions in square brackets are worked as stated after 2nd bracket.

Square two

Medium motif

(Make 15)

Each square uses 4 colours, A, B, C and D. Use at least one key colour in each square, and other colours randomly to create a fun effect.

1st round: With 4mm hook and A, make 4ch, 15tr in 4th ch from hook, ss in 3rd of 3ch.

2nd round: 4ch (counts as 1tr and 1ch), [1tr in next tr, 1ch] 15 times, ss in 3rd of 4ch.

3rd round: 3ch (counts as 1tr throughout), 2tr in first ch-sp, [1tr next tr, 2tr in next ch-sp] 15 times, ss in 3rd of 3ch. Fasten off A.

Join B in same place as ss.

4th round: 1ch, 1dc in same st, [3ch, miss 2tr, 1dc in next tr, 10ch, miss 2tr, 1dc in next tr, 3ch, miss 2tr, 1dc in next tr, 5ch, miss 2tr, 1dc in next tr] 4 times, omitting final dc, ss in first dc.

5th round: Ss in 3-ch-sp, 1ch, 1dc in same ch-sp, work 5tr, 3ch and 5tr in 10-ch-sp, [1dc in 3-ch-sp, 7tr in 5-ch-sp, 1dc in 3-ch-sp, work 5tr, 3ch and 5tr in 10-ch-sp] 3 times, 1dc in 3-ch-sp, 7tr in 5-ch-sp, ss in first dc. Fasten off B.

Join C in same place as ss.

6th round: 8ch (counts as 1tr and 5ch), miss 5tr, [work 1dc, 3ch and 1dc in 3-ch-sp, 5ch, miss 5tr, 1tr in next dc, 3ch, miss 3tr, 1dc in next tr, 3ch, miss 3tr, 1tr in next dc, 5ch, miss 5tr] 3 times, work 1dc, 3ch and 1dc in 3-ch-sp, 5ch, miss 5tr, 1tr in next dc, 3ch, miss 3tr, 1dc in next tr, 3ch, miss last 3tr, ss in 3rd of 8ch.

7th round: 3ch, 4tr in 5-ch-sp, *work 3tr, 3ch and 3tr in 3-ch-sp, 5tr in 5-ch-sp, [3tr in next 3-ch-sp] twice, 5tr in 5-ch-sp, repeat from * twice more, work 3tr, 3ch and 3tr in 3-ch-sp, 5tr in 5-ch-sp, [3tr in next 3-ch-sp] twice, ss in 3rd of 3ch.

Fasten off C.

Join D in same place as ss.

8th round: 1ch, 1dc in same st, 1dc in each tr and 3dc in each corner 3-ch-sp, ss in first dc.

Fasten off.

Measurements

The completed throw measures approximately 117 x 145cm (46 x 57in), including edging.

Materials

Bergere de France Ideal (40% wool, 30% acrylic, 30% polyamide) in 50g (125m) balls. Entire blanket requires the following:

Key colours: 3 balls in each of Meije (51253), Olivine (20754) and Vannerie (23316).
2 balls in each of Cyclamen (20555) and Danseuse (23026).

Other colours: 2 balls in each of Linaire (20933), Lievre (54695) and Beige Rose (35177).
1 ball in each of Myosotis (20841), Jaune (35166), Pinede (25324), Belladone (22375), Vitamine (24109), Cendre (24241), Persan (24257) and Sequoia (35168).

Joining and edging: 5 balls Everest (51220).
Size 4mm crochet hook.

Tension

Large motif measures approx. 24 x 24cm (9.4 x 9.4in), medium motif measures approx. 12 x 12cm (4.7 x 4.7in) and small motif measures approx. 6 x 6cm (2.3 x 2.3in); using 4mm hook.

Abbreviations

Ch, chain; **ch-sp**, chain space; **dc**, double crochet; **htr**, half treble; **tr**, treble; **sp**, space; **st**, stitch; **ss**, slip stitch; **yrh**, yarn over hook; **tr2tog**, work 2tr together thus: [yrh, insert hook in ch-sp indicated, yrh and pull through, yrh and pull through first 2 loops on hook] twice, yrh and pull through all 3 loops on hook; **tr3tog**, work 3tr together thus: [yrh, insert hook in ch-sp indicated, yrh and pull through, yrh and pull through first 2 loops on hook] 3 times.

Note

Yarn amounts are approximate. Instructions in square brackets are worked as stated after 2nd bracket.

Square three

Medium motif

(Make 16)

Work squares in 2, 3 or 4 colours, changing colour at the end of every round. On 3- or 4-colour squares, use colours in sequence. Use at least one key colour in each square, and other colours randomly.

1st round: With 4mm hook and first colour, make 6ch, [3tr, 2ch] 3 times in 6th ch from hook, 2tr in same place as before, ss in 3rd of 5ch. Fasten off.

Join new colour in any 2-ch-sp.

2nd round: 7ch (counts as 1tr and 4ch), 2tr in same 2-ch-sp, [1tr in each of next 3tr, work 2tr, 4ch and 2tr in next 2-ch-sp] 3 times, 1tr in each of next 3tr, 1tr in same 2-ch-sp at base of 7ch, ss in 3rd of 7ch. Fasten off.

Join new colour in any 4-ch-sp.

3rd round: 1ch, [5dc in 4-ch-sp, 1dc in each of next 3tr, insert hook in next tr, yrh and pull loop through, insert hook in st in round below same tr, yrh and pull loop through, yrh and pull through all 3 loops – spike st made, 1dc in each of next 3tr] 4 times, ss in first dc.
Fasten off.

Join new colour in same place as ss.

4th round: 3ch (counts as 1tr throughout), 1tr in next dc, [4ch, miss next dc, 1tr in each of next 11 sts] 3 times, 4ch, miss next dc, 1tr in each of last 9 sts, ss in 3rd of 3ch. Fasten off.

Join new colour in same place as ss.

5th round: 3ch, 1tr in next tr, [work 2tr, 4ch and 2tr in 4-ch-sp, 1tr in each of next 11 sts] 3 times, work 2tr, 4ch and 2tr in 4-ch-sp, 1tr in each of last 9 sts, ss in 3rd of 3ch. Fasten off.

Join new colour in same place as ss.

6th round: 1ch, 1dc in same st, 1dc in each of next 3tr, [5dc in 4-ch-sp, 1dc in each of next 4tr, spike st in next tr, 1dc in each of next 5tr, spike st in next tr, 1dc in each of next 4 sts] 3 times, 5dc in 4-ch-sp, 1dc in each of next 4tr, spike st in next tr, 1dc in each of next 5tr, spike st in last tr, ss in first dc. Fasten off.

Join new colour in same place as ss.

7th round: 3ch, 1tr in each of next 5dc, [4ch, miss 1dc, 1tr in each of next 19 sts] 3 times, 4ch, miss 1dc, 1tr in each of last 13 sts, ss in 3rd of 3ch. Fasten off.

Join new colour in same place as ss.

8th round: 3ch, 1tr in each of next 5tr, [work 2tr, 4ch and 2tr in 4-ch-sp, 1tr in each of next 19tr] 3 times, work 2tr, 4ch and 2tr in 4-ch-sp, 1tr in each of last 13tr, ss in 3rd of 3ch.
Fasten off.

Measurements

The completed throw measures approximately 117 x 145cm (46 x 57in), including edging.

Materials

Bergere de France Ideal (40% wool, 30% acrylic, 30% polyamide) in 50g (125m) balls. Entire blanket requires the following:

Key colours: 3 balls in each of Meije (51253), Olivine (20754) and Vannerie (23316).

2 balls in each of Cyclamen (20555) and Danseuse (23026).

Other colours: 2 balls in each of Linaire (20933), Lievre (54695) and Beige Rose (35177).

1 ball in each of Myosotis (20841), Jaune (35166), Pinede (25324), Belladone (22375), Vitamine (24109), Cendre (24241), Persan (24257) and Sequoia (35168).

Joining and edging: 5 balls Everest (51220).

Size 4mm crochet hook.

Tension

Large motif measures approx. 24 x 24cm (9.4 x 9.4in), medium motif measures approx. 12 x 12cm (4.7 x 4.7in) and small motif measures approx. 6 x 6cm (2.3 x 2.3in); using 4mm hook.

Abbreviations

Ch, chain; **ch-sp**, chain space; **dc**, double crochet; **htr**, half treble; **tr**, treble; **sp**, space; **st**, stitch; **ss**, slip stitch; **yrh**, yarn over hook; **tr2tog**, work 2tr together thus: [yrh, insert hook in ch-sp indicated, yrh and pull through, yrh and pull through first 2 loops on hook] twice, yrh and pull through all 3 loops on hook; **tr3tog**, work 3tr together thus: [yrh, insert hook in ch-sp indicated, yrh and pull through, yrh and pull through first 2 loops on hook] 3 times.

Note

Yarn amounts are approximate. Instructions in square brackets are worked as stated after 2nd bracket.

Square four

Medium motif

(Make 28)

Each square uses 4 colours, A, B, C and D. Use at least one of the key colours in each square, and other colours randomly.

1st round: With 4mm hook and A, make 4ch, 1tr in 4th ch from hook, 3ch, ss into 3rd ch from hook – picot worked, [3tr, picot] 7 times in same place as first tr, 1tr in same place as first tr, ss in top of first 3ch. Fasten off A.

Join B to centre tr of any 3-tr group.

2nd round: 1ch, 1dc in same st, 6ch, [1dc in centre tr of next 3-tr group, 6ch] 7 times, ss in first dc.

3rd round: 1ch, [work 3dc, 3ch, 1dc, 3ch and 3dc all in next 6-ch-sp, 9ch, work 3dc, 3ch, 1dc, 3ch and 3dc all in next 6-ch-sp] 4 times, ss to first dc. Fasten off B.

Join C to centre of any 9-ch-sp.

4th round: 1ch, [3dc in 9-ch-sp, 4ch, miss next 3-ch-sp, 1dc in next 3-ch-sp, 4ch, 1dc in next 3-ch-sp, 4ch, miss next 3-ch-sp] 4 times, ss in first dc.

5th round: 3ch (counts as 1tr), *work 1tr, 1ch, 1tr, 1ch and 1tr all in next dc, [1tr in next dc, 4tr in 4-ch-sp] 3 times, 1tr in next dc, repeat from * 3 times more, omitting 1tr at end of final repeat, ss in 3rd of 3ch.

6th round: 3ch, 1tr in next tr, [1tr in 1-ch-sp, work 1tr, 1ch, 1tr, 1ch and 1tr all in next tr, 1tr in 1-ch-sp, 1tr in each of next 18tr] 3 times, 1tr in 1-ch-sp, work 1tr, 1ch, 1tr, 1ch and 1tr all in next tr, 1tr in next ch-sp, 1tr in each of last 16tr, ss in 3rd of 3ch. Fasten off C.

Join D to same st as ss.

7th round: 1ch, 1dc in same st as join, 1dc in each of next 3tr, [1dc in 1-ch-sp, 3dc in next tr, 1dc in 1-ch-sp, 1dc in each of next 22tr] 3 times, 1dc in 1-ch-sp, 3dc in next tr, 1dc in 1-ch-sp, 1dc in each of last 18tr, ss in first dc. Fasten off.

Square five and six

Small motif 1

(Make 54)

Each square uses 3 colours, A, B and C. Use at least one key colour in each square, and other colours randomly.

1st round: With 4mm hook and A, make 4ch, 15tr in 4th ch from hook, ss in 3rd of 3ch – 16 sts.

2nd round: 2ch (counts as 1htr), 1htr next st, work 2tr, 2ch and 2tr all in next st, [1htr in each of next 3 sts, work 2tr, 2ch and 2tr all in next st] 3 times, 1htr in last st, ss in 2nd of 2ch.

Fasten off A. Join B in same place as ss.

3rd round: 4ch (counts as 1tr and 1ch), miss next st, 1tr in next st, 1ch, miss next st, *work 2tr, 2ch and 2tr all in next 2-ch-sp, [1ch, miss next st, 1tr in next st] 3 times, 1ch, miss next st, repeat from * twice more, work 2tr, 2ch and 2tr all in last 2-ch-sp, 1ch, miss next st, 1tr in next st, 1ch, miss last st, ss in 3rd of 4ch.

Fasten off B.

Join C in same place as ss.

4th round: 1ch, 1dc into each tr and ch-sp, working 1dc, 1ch and 1dc all in each corner 2-ch-sp, ss in first dc.

Fasten off.

Small motif 2

(Make 10)

Each square uses 3 colours, A, B and C. Use at least one key colour in each square, and other colours randomly to create a unique effect.

1st round: With 4mm hook and A, make 4ch, 23tr in 4th ch from hook, ss in 3rd of 3ch – 24 sts.

2nd round: 6ch (counts as 1dc and 5ch), miss next 2tr, [1dc in next tr, 5ch, miss next 2tr] 7 times, ss in first of 6ch.

Fasten off A.

Join B in any 5-ch-sp.

3rd round: 3ch, tr2tog in 5-ch-sp, 3ch, [tr3tog, 3ch] twice in same 5-ch-sp, 1dc in next 5-ch-sp, 3ch, *[tr3tog, 3ch] 3 times in next 5-ch-sp, 1dc in next 5-ch-sp, 3ch, repeat from * twice more, ss in top of tr2tof. Fasten off B.

Join C in same place as ss.

4th round: 1ch, 1dc in tr2tog, [2dc in next 3-ch-sp, 1dc, 1ch and 1dc all in next tr3tog, 2dc in next 3-ch-sp, 1dc in next tr3tog, 2dc in next 3-ch-sp, 1dc in next dc, 2dc in next 3-ch-sp, 1dc in next tr3tog] 4 times, omitting final dc, ss in first dc. Fasten off.

Measurements

The completed throw measures approximately 117 x 145cm (46 x 57in), including edging.

Materials

Bergere de France Ideal (40% wool, 30% acrylic, 30% polyamide) in 50g (125m) balls. Entire blanket requires the following:

Key colours: 3 balls in each of Meije (51253), Olivine (20754) and Vannerie (23316).

2 balls in each of Cyclamen (20555) and Danseuse (23026).

Other colours: 2 balls in each of Linaire (20933), Lievre (54695) and Beige Rose (35177).

1 ball in each of Myosotis (20841), Jaune (35166), Pinede (25324), Belladone (22375), Vitamine (24109), Cendre (24241), Persan (24257) and Sequoia (35168).

Joining and edging: 5 balls Everest (51220).

Size 4mm crochet hook.

Tension

Large motif measures approx. 24 x 24cm (9.4 x 9.4in), medium motif measures approx. 12 x 12cm (4.7 x 4.7in) and small motif measures approx. 6 x 6cm (2.3 x 2.3in); using 4mm hook.

Abbreviations

Ch, chain; **ch-sp**, chain space; **dc**, double crochet; **htr**, half treble; **tr**, treble; **sp**, space; **st**, stitch; **ss**, slip stitch; **yrh**, yarn over hook; **tr2tog**, work 2tr together thus: [yrh, insert hook in ch-sp indicated, yrh and pull through, yrh and pull through first 2 loops on hook] twice, yrh and pull through all 3 loops on hook; **tr3tog**, work 3tr together thus: [yrh, insert hook in ch-sp indicated, yrh and pull through, yrh and pull through first 2 loops on hook] 3 times.

Note

Yarn amounts are approximate. Instructions in square brackets are worked as stated after 2nd bracket.

Measurements

The completed throw measures approximately 117 x 145cm (46 x 57in), including edging.

Materials

Bergere de France Ideal (40% wool, 30% acrylic, 30% polyamide) in 50g (125m) balls. Entire blanket requires the following:
Key colours: 3 balls in each of Meije (51253), Olivine (20754) and Vannerie (23316).
2 balls in each of Cyclamen (20555) and Danseuse (23026).
Other colours: 2 balls in each of Linaire (20933), Lievre (54695) and Beige Rose (35177).
1 ball in each of Myosotis (20841), Jaune (35166), Pinede (25324), Belladone (22375), Vitamine (24109), Cendre (24241), Persan (24257) and Sequoia (35168).
Joining and edging: 5 balls Everest (51220).
Size 4mm crochet hook.

Tension

Large motif measures approx. 24 x 24cm (9.4 x 9.4in), medium motif measures approx. 12 x 12cm (4.7 x 4.7in) and small motif measures approx. 6 x 6cm (2.3 x 2.3in); using 4mm hook.

Abbreviations

Ch, chain; **ch-sp**, chain space; **dc**, double crochet; **htr**, half treble; **tr**, treble; **sp**, space; **st**, stitch; **ss**, slip stitch; **yrh**, yarn over hook; **tr2tog**, work 2tr together thus: [yrh, insert hook in ch-sp indicated, yrh and pull through, yrh and pull through first 2 loops on hook] twice, yrh and pull through all 3 loops on hook; **tr3tog**, work 3tr together thus: [yrh, insert hook in ch-sp indicated, yrh and pull through, yrh and pull through first 2 loops on hook] 3 times.

Note

Yarn amounts are approximate. Instructions in square brackets are worked as stated after 2nd bracket.

Put it together

To make up

Follow the diagram below for positioning of squares to create a fun, jumbled look.

To join small squares

With wrong sides together, join Everest to corner, 1ch, join with dc in back loop only of each st to corner. Fasten off.

To join medium and large squares

With wrong sides together, join Everest to corner of first square, 2ch, 1htr in corner of second square, [1ch, miss 1 st on first square and work 1htr in next st, 1ch, miss 1 st on second square and work 1htr in next st] to next corner, noting that sts may not match up equally and to even squares out, it may be necessary to miss an extra st occasionally.
Fasten off.

Edging

With right side facing, join Everest to one corner of throw, 1ch, 1dc in corner, [miss 2 sts, 5tr in next st, miss 2 sts, 1dc in next st] around outer edge, omitting 1dc at end, ss in first dc.
Fasten off.

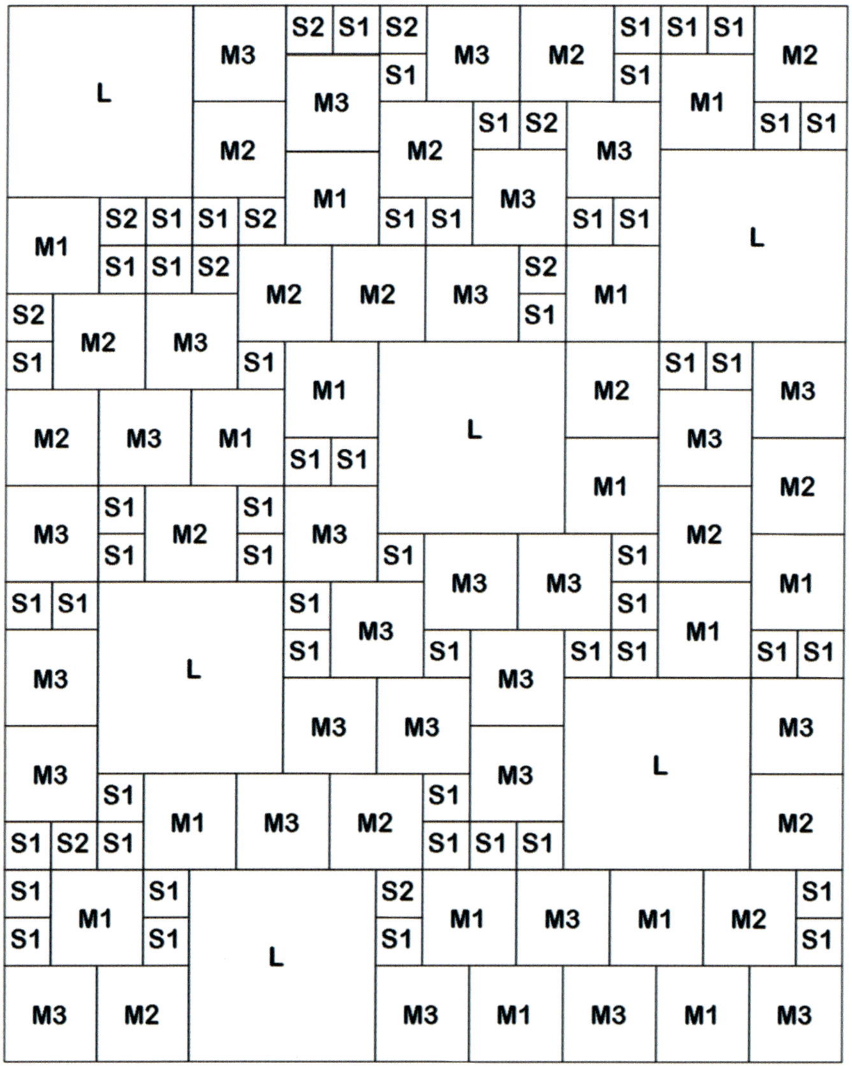

KEY

L – large motif
M1 – medium motif 1
M2 – medium motif 2
M3 – medium motif 3
S1 – small motif 1
S2 – small motif 2

☐ EASY PEASY
☑ A BIT MORE TRICKY
☐ HARD-ISH
☐ QUITE A CHALLENGE

Blanket stitching

Worked in trebles with dc and a shell-edged border in a colourful palette, this granny square blanket would make a stunning on-trend addition for your home

Measurements

Approximately 124 x 180cm/ 48¾ x 70¾in.

Materials

For complete blanket: 9 x 100g (280m) balls of Hayfield Bonus DK (100% acrylic) in Aran (993); 2 balls in each of Claret (841) and Cupid (944); 1 ball in each of Emerald (916), Lilac (959), Bright Purple (828), Petrol (829), Primrose (957), Powder Blue (960) and Mint (956). Size 4mm crochet hook.

Tension

One complete square measures 20 x 20cm, using 4mm hook.

Abbreviations

Ch, chain; **dc**, double crochet; **tr**, treble; **st(s)**, stitch(es); **ss**, slip stitch; **ch sp**, chain space.

Note

Yarn amounts are based on average requirements and are therefore approximate. Instructions in square brackets are worked as stated after 2nd bracket.

Square A

(Make 8)

With 4mm hook and Lilac, make 4ch and join with a ss to form a ring.

1st round: 3ch (counts as 1tr), 2tr in ring, 3ch, [3tr in ring, 3ch] 3 times, ss in 3rd of 3ch.

2nd round: Ss along and into 3ch-sp (counts as 1tr), work 2tr, 3ch and 3tr in same ch-sp for corner, [1ch, work 3tr, 3ch and 3tr in next ch-sp] 3 times, 1ch, ss in 3rd of 3ch. Fasten off.

3rd round: Join in Aran to any corner ch-sp, 3ch (counts as 1tr), work 2tr, 3ch and 3tr in same ch-sp, 1ch, 3tr in next 1ch-sp, [1ch, work 3tr, 3ch and 3tr in next corner ch-sp, 1ch, 3tr in next 1ch-sp] 3 times, 1ch, ss in 3rd of 3ch. Fasten off.

4th round: Join Bright Purple to any corner ch-sp, 3ch (counts as 1tr), work 2tr, 3ch and 3tr in same ch-sp, 1ch, [3tr in next 1ch-sp, 1ch] twice, *work 3tr, 3ch and 3tr in next corner ch-sp, 1ch, [3tr in next 1ch-sp, 1ch] twice, repeat from * twice more, ss in 3rd of 3ch. Fasten off.

5th round: Join Aran to any corner ch-sp, 3ch (counts as 1tr), work 2tr, 3ch and 3tr in same ch-sp, 1ch, [3tr in next 1ch-sp, 1ch] 3 times, *work 3tr, 3ch and 3tr in next corner ch-sp, 1ch, [3tr in next 1ch-sp, 1ch] 3 times, repeat from * twice more, ss in 3rd of 3ch.

6th round: Ss along and into corner ch-sp, 3ch (counts as 1tr), work 2tr, 3ch and 3tr in same ch-sp, 1ch, [3tr in next 1ch-sp, 1ch] to corner ch-sp, *work 3tr, 3ch and 3tr in corner ch-sp, 1ch, [3tr in next 1ch-sp, 1ch] to corner ch-sp, repeat from * twice more, ss in 3rd of 3ch.

7th round: As 6th round.

8th round: As 6th round, but do not break off Aran.

9th round: As 6th round or as joining round of joining squares.

Square B, C, D or E

Breaking off colours at end of every round and joining new colour to any 3ch-sp at corner at beginning of following round, work 1st to 9th rounds as square A, using colours as follows:

Square B with Mint centre (make 5): Work 1 round in each of Mint, Petrol, Cupid, Aran, Lilac, Aran, Bright Purple and 2 rounds in Aran.

Square C with Primrose centre (make 12): Work 1 round in each of Primrose, Petrol, Powder Blue, Cupid, Claret, Aran, Emerald and 2 rounds in Aran.

Square D with Aran centre (make 10): Work 1 round in each of Aran, Mint, Petrol, Lilac, Cupid, Aran, Claret and 2 rounds in Aran.

Square E with Claret centre (make 4): Work 1 round in each of Claret, Mint, Petrol, Aran, Lilac, Aran, Cupid and 2 rounds in Aran.

Join squares

Following chart for placement, beginning at bottom corner and working in diagonal lines, make and join squares as required thus:

Joining round: Ss along and into ch-sp at corner, 3ch (counts as 1tr), work 2tr, 3ch and 3tr in same ch-sp, 1ch, [3tr in next 1ch-sp, 1ch] 7 times, 3tr in ch-sp at corner, 1ch, place wrong sides of two squares together and with working square at front, ss into corner ch-sp on square at back – corner join made, *1ch, 3tr in same corner ch-sp on square at front, [ss in next ch-sp on square at back, 3tr in next ch-sp on square at front] to next corner ch-sp, 1ch, 3tr in corner ch-sp on square at front, 1ch, ss in corner ch-sp or in join on square at back, repeat from * once more if joining square on two sides, then complete square at front as 6th round of square A. Fasten off.

Triangular inserts

With 4mm hook and Aran, make 4ch and join with a ss to form a ring.

1st row: 4ch (counts as 1tr and 1ch), work 3tr, 3ch, 3tr, 1ch and 1tr in ring, turn.

2nd row: 4ch (counts as 1tr and 1ch), 3tr in next 1ch-sp, 1ch, work 3tr, 3ch and 3tr in 3ch-sp, 1ch, 3tr in 4th of 4ch, 1ch, 1tr in 3rd of 4ch, turn.

3rd row: 4ch (counts as 1tr and 1ch), [3tr in next 1ch-sp, 1ch] twice, work 3tr, 3ch

and 3tr in 3ch-sp, 1ch, 3tr in next 1ch-sp, 1ch, 3tr in 4th of 4ch, 1ch, 1tr in 3rd of 4ch, turn.

4th row: 4ch (counts as 1tr and 1ch), [3tr in next 1ch-sp, 1ch] 3 times, work 3tr, 3ch and 3tr in 3ch-sp, 1ch, [3tr in next 1ch-sp, 1ch] twice, 3tr in 4th of 4ch, 1ch, 1tr in 3rd of 4ch, turn.

5th row: 4ch (counts as 1tr and 1ch), [3tr in next 1ch-sp, 1ch] to 3ch-sp at corner, work 3tr, 3ch and 3tr in 3ch-sp, 1ch, [3tr in next 1ch-sp, 1ch] to 4ch at end, 3tr in 4th of 4ch, 1ch, 1tr in 3rd of 4ch, turn.

6th to 8th rows: As 5th row.

9th (joining) row: 3ch, ss into corner ch-sp on square of main part, [3tr in ch-sp on triangle, ss in next 1ch-sp on square] 8 times, 3tr in corner ch-sp on triangle, 1ch, ss in corner join on main part, 1ch, 3tr in same ch-sp on triangle, ss in next ch-sp of following square on main part, [3tr in next ch-sp on triangle, ss in next ch-sp on square] 7 times, 3tr in 4th of 4ch on triangle, ss in corner ch-sp on square, 1tr in 3rd of 4ch on triangle. Fasten off. Make and join five triangles to each long edge of blanket, and three to each short edge.

Corner triangle

With 4mm hook and Aran, make 4ch and join with a ss to form a ring.

1st row: 4ch (counts as 1tr and 1ch), work 3tr, 1ch and 1tr in ring, turn.

2nd row: 4ch (counts as 1tr and 1ch), 3tr in 1ch-sp, 1ch, 3tr in 4th of 4ch, 1ch, 1tr in 3rd of 4ch, turn.

3rd row: 4ch (counts as 1tr and 1ch), [3tr in next 1ch-sp, 1ch] twice, 3tr in 4th of 4ch, 1ch, 1tr in 3rd of 4ch, turn.

4th row: 4ch (counts as 1tr and 1ch), [3tr in next 1ch-sp, 1ch] to 4ch at end, 3tr in 4th of 4ch, 1ch, 1tr in 3rd of 4ch, turn.

5th to 8th rows: As 4th row.

9th (joining) row: 3ch, ss in corner ch-sp on square of main part, [3tr in next 1ch-sp on triangle, ss in next ch-sp on square] 8 times, 3tr in 4th of 4ch on triangle, ss in corner ch-sp on square, 1tr in 3rd of 4ch on triangle. Fasten off.

Border

1st round: With right side facing, join Aran to ring at one corner triangle, 1ch (does not count as a st), [3dc in corner, work 299dc along long edge to next corner, 3dc in corner, 197dc along short edge to next corner] twice, ss in first dc – 1004dc. Work 2 rounds in dc, working 1ch at beginning, 3dc at each corner and ss to first dc at end of every round.

Next round: Ss along to corner st, 4ch (counts as 1tr and 1ch), 1tr in base of 4ch, *1ch, 1tr in next st, [1ch, miss next st, 1tr in next st] to corner st, 1ch, work 1tr, 1ch and 1tr in corner st, repeat from * twice more, 1ch, 1tr in next st, [1ch, miss next st, 1tr in next st] to end, 1ch, ss in 3rd of 4ch.

Next 2 rounds: Ss along and into corner ch-sp, 4ch (counts as 1tr and 1ch), 1tr in same ch-sp, *[1ch, 1tr in next tr] to corner ch-sp, 1ch, work 1tr, 1ch and 1tr in corner ch-sp, repeat from * twice more, [1ch, 1tr in next tr] to end, 1ch, ss in 3rd of 4ch.

Next round: 1ch (counts as 1dc), 3dc in first ch-sp, *[work 1dc in each st] to corner ch-sp, 3dc in corner ch-sp, repeat from * twice more, [1dc in each st] to end, ss in 1ch. Work 2 rounds in dc as before.

Shell round: Ss to corner st, 3ch, 4tr in same st, miss 2 sts, 1dc in next st, [miss 2 sts, 5tr in next st, miss next 2 sts, 1dc in next st] to last 2 sts, miss 2 sts, ss in top of 3ch. Fasten off and neaten ends.

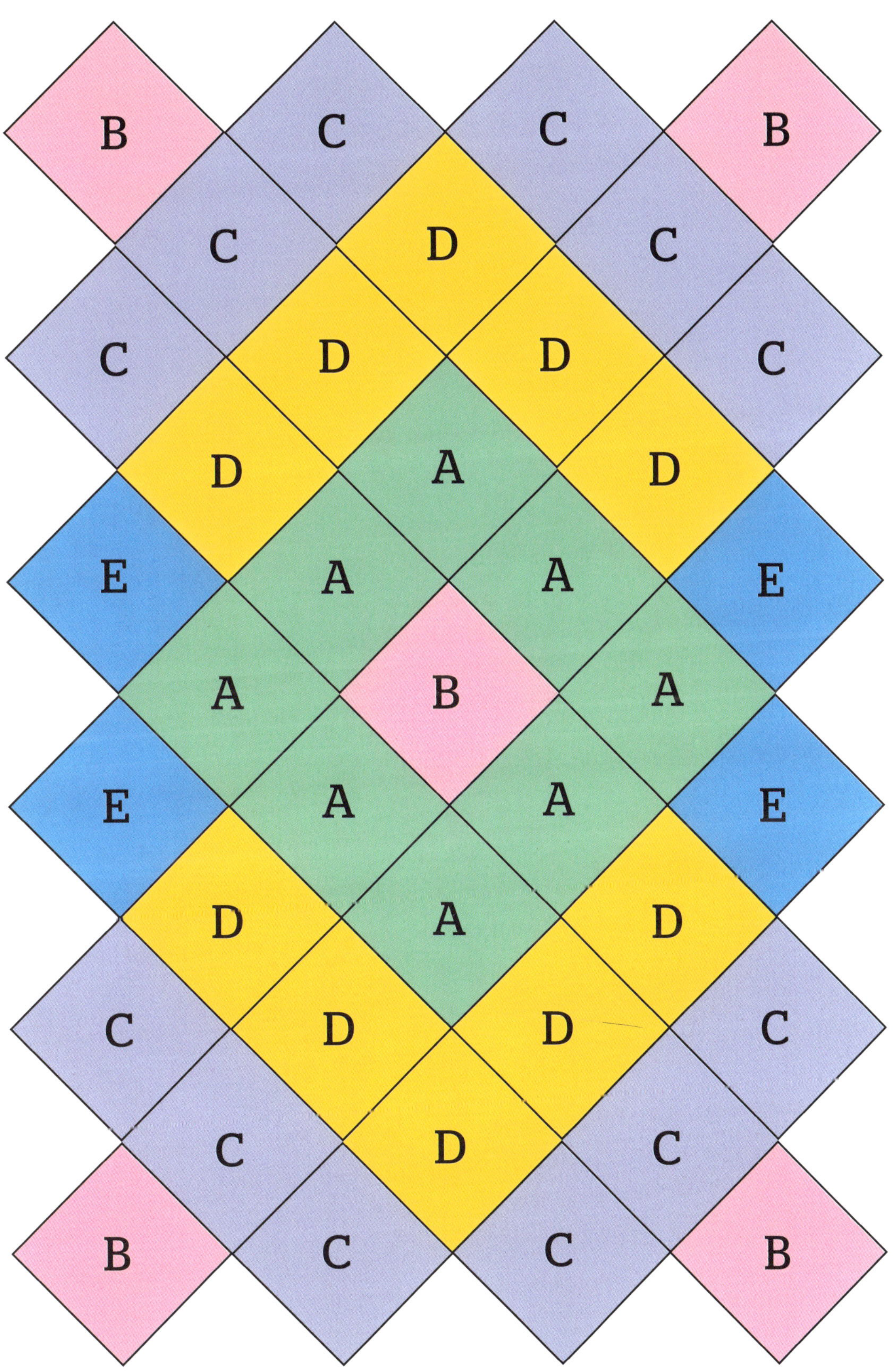
B
C
C
B
C
D
C
C
D
D
C
D
A
D
E
A
A
E
A
B
A
E
A
A
E
D
A
D
C
D
D
C
C
D
C
B
C
C
B

Portuguese tile blanket

A gorgeous crochet throw for your home, inspired by the ornate tiles of Portugal

- ☐ EASY PEASY
- ☑ A BIT MORE TRICKY
- ☐ HARD-ISH
- ☐ QUITE A CHALLENGE

Measurements

When complete, the blanket will measure approximately 104 x 104cm (41 x 41in).

Materials

For complete blanket: 1 x 100g (295m) ball of Stylecraft Special DK (100% acrylic) in each of White (1001), Aster (1003), Cloud Blue (1019), Royal (1117), Duck Egg (1820) and Mustard (1823).
Size 4mm crochet hook.

Tension

Each square measures approximately 14 x 14cm (5½ x 5½in), using 4mm hook.

Abbreviations

Ch, chain; **st(s)**, stitch(es); **dc**, double crochet; **tr**, treble crochet; **htr**, half treble crochet; **dtr**, double treble crochet; **ss**, slip stitch; **yrh**, yarn round hook; **3tr-cl**, 3 treble cluster thus: yrh [insert hook into st indicated, yrh, pull up loop, yrh, pull hook through first 2 loops on hook, leaving remaining loops on hook] 3 times (4 loops remain on hook), yrh and pull through all loops on hook; **beg 3tr-cl**, beginning 3 treble cluster thus: 2ch, yrh [insert hook into st indicated, yrh, pull up loop, yrh, pull hook through first 2 loops on hook, leaving remaining loops on hook] 2 times (3 loops remain on hook), yrh and pull through all loops on hook; **ch-sp(s)**, chain space(s).

Note

Yarn amounts are based on average requirements and are therefore approximate. Instructions in square brackets are worked as stated after 2nd bracket.

Square one

(Make 9)

With 4mm hook and Mustard, make 5ch and ss to first ch to make a ring (do not ch to begin 1st round as it makes a too-obvious difference to your circle).

1st round: 8htr into ring, ss in first htr – 8 sts.

Fasten off Mustard.

2nd round: Join Duck Egg with a ss to any st, beg 3tr-cl in same st, [3ch, 3tr-cl in next st] to last st, 3ch, ss to top of beg 3tr-cl – 8 3tr-cl and 8 3-ch-sps.

Fasten off Duck Egg.

3rd round: Join White with a ss to any 3-ch-sp, 2ch (counts as 1htr), [1tr, 1dtr, 1tr, 1htr] in same 3-ch-sp, 1dc in top of next 3tr-cl, *[1htr, 1tr, 1dtr, 1tr, 1htr] in next 3-ch-sp, 1dc in top of next 3tr-cl; repeat from * to end, ss to top of beginning 2ch – 48 sts.

Fasten off White.

4th round: Join Royal with a ss to any dtr, 1ch (does not count as a st), [1dc in dtr, 6ch, miss next 5 sts] to end, ss to first dc – 8 dc and 8 6-ch-sps.

5th round: 1ch (does not count as a st), [7dc in next 6-ch-sp, 1dc in next dc] to end, ss in first dc – 64 sts.

Fasten off Royal.

6th round: Join Cloud Blue with a ss to a dc that was worked in a dc from 4th round, 3ch (counts as 1tr), 1tr in each of next 14 sts, [2dtr, 3ch, 2dtr] in next st, *1tr into each of next 15 sts, [2dtr, 3ch, 2dtr] in next st; repeat from * twice more, ss to top of beginning 3ch – 76 sts and 4 3-ch-sps.

Fasten off Cloud Blue.

7th round: Join Aster with a ss to corner 3-ch-sp, 3ch (counts as 1tr), [1tr, 3ch, 2tr] in same 3-ch-sp, *1tr in back loop of each of next 19 sts, [2tr, 3ch, 2tr] in next 3-ch-sp; repeat from * twice more, 1tr in back loop of each of next 19 sts, ss to top of beginning 3ch – 92 sts and 4 3-ch-sps.

Fasten off and weave in all ends.

BEGIN BY WORKING TREBLE STITCHES INTO A CHAIN RING

Tension

Each square measures approximately 14 x 14cm/ 5½ x 5½in, using 4mm hook.

Abbreviations

Ch, chain; **st(s)**, stitches; **dc**, double crochet; **tr**, treble crochet; **htr**, half treble crochet; **dtr**, double treble crochet; **ss**, slip stitch; **yrh**, yarn round hook; **5tr-cl**, 5 treble cluster thus: yrh [insert hook into st indicated, yrh, pull up loop, yrh, pull hook through first 2 loops on hook, leaving remaining loops on hook] 5 times (6 loops remain on hook), yrh and pull through all loops on hook; **beg 5tr-cl**, beginning 5 treble cluster thus: 2ch, yrh [insert hook into st indicated, yrh, pull up loop, yrh, pull hook through first 2 loops on hook, leaving remaining loops on hook] 4 times (5 loops remain on hook), yrh and pull through all loops on hook; **ch-sp(s)**, chain space(s).

Note

Yarn amounts are based on average requirements and are therefore approximate. Instructions in square brackets are worked as stated after 2nd bracket.

Layout for sewing squares together

1	2	1
2	1	2
1	2	1

JOIN BY HOLDING THE SQUARES WITH RIGHT SIDES TOGETHER AND EITHER SS OR WHIP STITCH THROUGH BACK LOOPS OF EACH SQUARE TO FORM A NEAT JOIN

Square two

(Make 8)
With 4mm hook and Aster, make 8ch and ss to first ch to make a ring.

1st round: 3ch (counts as 1tr), 2tr into ring, 1ch, [3tr, 1ch] 7 times into ring, ss to top of beginning 3ch – 24 tr and 8 1-ch-sps.
Fasten off Aster.

2nd round: Join Cloud Blue with a ss to any 1-ch-sp, beg 5tr-cl in same 1-ch-sp, 6ch, [5tr-cl in next 1-ch-sp, 6ch] to end, ss to top of beg 5tr-cl – 8 5tr-cl and 8 6-ch-sps.
Fasten off Cloud Blue.

3rd round: Join Royal with a ss to top of any 5tr-cl, 1ch (does not count as a st), 1dc in same 5tr-cl, 7tr in next 6-ch-sp, [1dc in next 5tr-cl, 7tr in next 6-ch-sp] to end, ss to first dc – 64 sts.
Fasten off Royal.

4th round: Join White with a ss to any dc, 4ch (counts as 1tr and 1ch), [1tr, 1ch] 3 times in same dc, *[1dtr, 1ch, 1dtr, 3ch, 1dtr, 1ch, 1dtr, 1ch] in next dc, [1tr, 1ch] 4 times in next dc; repeat from * twice more, [1dtr, 1ch, 1dtr, 3ch, 1dtr, 1ch, 1dtr, 1ch] in last dc, ss to 3rd ch of beginning 4ch – 16 dtr, 16 tr, 28 1-ch-sp and 4 3-ch-sps.
Fasten off White.

5th round: Join Duck Egg to any 3-ch-sp, 3ch (counts as 1tr), [1tr, 3ch, 2tr] in same 3-ch-sp, 1ch, [1htr, 1ch] in each of next 7 1-ch-sps, *[2tr, 3ch, 2tr] in next 3-ch-sp, 1ch, [1htr, 1ch] in each of next 7 1-ch-sps; repeat from * twice more, ss to top of beginning 3ch – 16 tr, 28 htr, 32 1-ch-sps and 4 3-ch-sps.
Fasten off Duck Egg.

6th round: Join Mustard with a ss to any 3-ch-sp, 3ch (counts as 1tr), [1tr, 3ch, 2tr] in same 3-ch-sp, 1tr in each st and 1-ch-sp to next 3-ch-sp, *[2tr, 3ch, 2tr] in next 3-ch-sp, 1tr in each st and 1-ch-sp to next 3-ch-sp; repeat from * twice more, ss to top of beginning 3ch – 92 sts and 4 3-ch-sps. Fasten off and weave in ends. Join together 9 squares of squares 1 and 2 in the following layout and put the remainder of the squares aside as you will need them later.

Inner edging

To make

This part is worked around the large square made up of the 9 smaller squares.

1st round: With 4mm hook, join White with a ss to any corner 3-ch-sp of the large square, 3ch (counts as 1tr here and throughout pattern), [1tr, 3ch, 2tr] in same 3-ch-sp, *[1ch, miss next st, 1tr in next st] 11 times, 1ch, miss next st, 1tr in ch-sp before the joining seam of next square, 1ch, 1tr in ch-sp after joining seam**; repeat from * to ** once more, [1ch, miss next st, 1tr in next st] 11 times, 1ch, miss next st, [2tr, 3ch, 2tr] in next 3-ch-sp***; repeat from * to *** another 3 times but on the last repeat omit the last [2tr, 3ch, 2tr], ss to top of beginning 3ch – 41 tr and 38 1-ch-sps along each side and a 3-ch-sp in each corner.

2nd round: Ss in next tr and ss into corner 3-ch-sp, 3ch, *[1tr, 3ch, 2tr] in same 3-ch-sp, 1ch, miss next 2 tr and 1-ch-sp, [shell in next 1-ch-sp, miss next 1-ch-sp, 1dc in next 1-ch-sp, miss next 1-ch-sp] 9 times, shell in next 1-ch-sp, 1ch, miss next 2 tr, [2tr, 3ch, 2tr] in next corner 3-ch-sp; repeat from * another 3 times but on the last repeat omit the last [2tr, 3ch, 2tr], ss to top of beginning 3ch – 10 shells, 9 dc, 4 tr and 2 1-ch-sps along each side and a 3-ch-sp in each corner.
Fasten off White.

3rd round: Join Duck Egg with a ss to any 3-ch-sp at corner, 3ch, [1tr, 3ch, 2tr] in same 3-ch-sp, miss 2 tr, *[1tr, 3ch, 1tr] in first 1-ch-sp, [6ch, miss shell, [1tr, 3ch, 1tr] in next dc] until the last shell and 1-ch-sp, 6ch, miss shell, [1tr, 3ch, 1tr] in last 1-ch-sp, miss 2 tr, [2tr, 3ch, 2tr] in corner 3-ch-sp; repeat from * another 3 times but on the last repeat omit the last [2tr, 3ch, 2tr], ss to top of 3ch – 11 3-ch-sps and 10 6-ch-sps along each side and a 3-ch-sp in each corner.

4th round: Ss in next tr and ss into corner 3-ch-sp, 3ch, [1tr, 3ch, 2tr] in same 3-ch-sp, 1ch, miss 2 tr, *[shell in next 3-ch-sp, 1dc over next 6-ch-sp and into centre tr of shell 2 rounds below] to last 3-ch-sp, shell in last 3-ch-sp, 1ch, [2tr, 3ch, 2tr] in next corner 3-ch-sp; repeat from * another 3 times but on the last repeat omit the last [2tr, 3ch, 2tr], ss to top of beginning 3ch – 11 shells, 10 dc, 4 tr and 2 1-ch-sps along each side and a 3-ch-sp in each corner.
Fasten off Duck Egg.

5th to 12th rounds: Repeat 3rd and 4th rounds once in Mustard, once in Aster, once in Cloud Blue and once in Royal – 15 shells, 14 dc, 4 tr and 2 1-ch-sps along each side and a 3-ch-sp in each corner.

13th round: Join White with a ss to any 3-ch-sp at corner, 3ch, [1tr, 3ch, 2tr] in same 3-ch-sp, *[1tr, 3ch, 1tr] in next 1-ch-sp, 3ch, 1dc in centre tr of next shell, 3ch; repeat from * to 1-ch-sp before corner, [1tr, 3ch, 1tr] in 1-ch-sp, [2tr, 3ch, 2tr] in corner 3-ch-sp**; repeat from * to ** another 3 times but on the last repeat omit the last [2tr, 3ch, 2tr], ss to top of beginning 3ch – 32 tr, 46 3-ch-sps and 15 dc along each side and a 3-ch-sp in each corner.

14th round: Ss in next tr and ss into corner 3-ch-sp, 3ch, [2tr, 3ch, 3tr] in same 3-ch-sp, miss 2 tr, *[3tr in next 3-ch-sp, 2tr in next 3-ch-sp] to next corner 3-ch-sp, [3tr, 3ch, 3tr] in corner 3-ch-sp; repeat from * another 3 times but on the last repeat omit the last [3tr, 3ch, 3tr], ss to top of beginning 3ch – 121 sts along each side and a 3-ch-sp in each corner.
Fasten off the White and then weave in the ends.

Measurements

When complete, the blanket will measure approximately 104 x 104cm (41 x 41in).

Size of blanket after completing inner edging is approximately 72 x 72cm (28¼ x 28¼in).

Tension

2.5 shells and 10 rounds, to 10 x 10cm/4 x 4in, over pattern, using 4mm hook.

Abbreviations

Ch, chain; **st(s)**, stitches; **dc**, double crochet; **sp**, space; **tr**, treble crochet; **ss**, slip stitch; **shell**, work shell in same st or sp, thus: [1tr, 1ch] 4 times, 1tr; **ch-sp(s)**, chain space(s).

Note

Yarn amounts are based on average requirements and are therefore approximate. Instructions in square brackets are worked as stated after 2nd bracket.

Tension

2.5 shells and 10 rounds, to 10 x 10cm/4 x 4in, over pattern, using 4mm hook.

Abbreviations

Ch, chain; **st(s)**, stitches; **dc**, double crochet; **tr**, treble crochet; **htr**, half treble crochet; **dtr**, double treble crochet; **ss**, slip stitch; **yrh**, yarn round hook; **3dtr-cl**, 3 double treble cluster thus: yrh twice, [insert hook into st indicated, yrh, pull up loop, (yrh, pull hook through first 2 loops on hook) twice, leaving remaining loops on hook] 3 times (4 loops remain on hook), yrh and pull through all loops on hook; **beg 3dtr-cl**, beginning 3 double treble cluster thus: 3ch, yrh twice, [insert hook into st indicated, yrh, pull up loop, (yrh, pull hook through first 2 loops on hook) twice, leaving remaining loops on hook] 2 times (3 loops remain on hook), yrh and pull through all loops on hook; **ch-sp(s)**, chain space(s); **Vst**, V stitch thus: [1tr, 1ch, 1tr] in same st or sp.

Note

Yarn amounts are based on average requirements and are therefore approximate. Instructions in square brackets are worked as stated after 2nd bracket.

Square four

(Make 8)

With 4mm hook and White, make 5ch and join to first ch with a ss to make a ring.

1st round: 4ch (counts as 1tr, 1ch), [1tr in ring, 1ch] 7 times, ss to 3rd of beginning 4ch – 8 tr and 8 1-ch-sps. Fasten off White.

2nd round: Join Royal with a ss to any 1-ch-sp, [4ch, 1dc in next 1-ch-sp] to end, ss to first of beginning 4ch – 8 dc and 8 4-ch-sps. Fasten off Royal.

3rd round: Join Duck Egg with a ss to any 4-ch-sp, [beg 3dtr-cl, 3ch, 3dtr-cl] in same 4-ch-sp, 3ch, *[3dtr-cl, 3ch, 3dtr-cl] in next 4-ch-sp, 3ch; repeat from * to end, ss in top of beginning 3dtr-cl – 16 3dtr-cl and 16 3-ch-sps. Fasten off Duck Egg.

4th round: Join Mustard with a ss to any 3-ch-sp, 2ch (counts as 1htr), 2htr in same 3-ch-sp, 1ch, [3htr in next 3-ch-sp, 1ch] to end, ss to top of beginning 2ch – 48 htr and 16 1-ch-sps. Fasten off Mustard.

5th round: Join Aster with a ss to any 1-ch-sp, 3ch (counts as 1tr), 2tr in same 3-ch-sp, 1ch, [3tr in next 1-ch-sp, 1ch] twice, *[3dtr, 3ch, 3dtr] in next 1-ch-sp, 1ch, [3tr in next 1-ch-sp, 1ch] 3 times; repeat from * twice more, [3dtr, 3ch, 3dtr] in next 1-ch-sp, 1ch, ss to top of beginning 3ch – 36 tr, 24 dtr, 16 1-ch-sps and 4 3-ch-sps.
Fasten off Aster.

6th round: Join Cloud Blue to any corner 3-ch-sp, 3ch (counts as 1tr), [1tr, 3ch, 2tr] in same 3-ch-sp, 1tr in each st and in each 1-ch-sp to next corner 3-ch-sp, *[2tr, 3ch, 2tr] in corner 3-ch-sp, 1tr in each st and in each 1-ch-sp to next corner 3-ch-sp; repeat from * twice more, ss to top of beginning 3ch – 92 sts and 4 3-ch-sps.
Fasten off and weave in ends.

Square five

(Make 8)
With 4mm hook and Cloud Blue, make 4ch and join to first ch with a ss to make a ring. Do not start 1st round with 3ch, as it makes a too obvious difference to your circle.

1st round: 8tr into ring, ss in first tr to join – 8 sts.
Fasten off Cloud Blue.

2nd round: Join Aster with a ss to any tr, [4ch, miss 1 st, 1dc in next st] to end, working the last dc in the same st as the ss join, ss in first of beginning 4ch – 4 dc and 4 4-ch-sps.

3rd round: *[1dc, 1htr, 1tr, 1htr, 1dc] in next 4-ch-sp, 1dc in next dc; repeat from * to end, ss in first dc – 24 sts.
Fasten off Aster.

4th round: Join Mustard with a ss to any tr, [3ch, miss next 2 sts, Vst in next st, 3ch, miss next 2 sts, 1dc in next st] to end, ss in first of beginning 3ch – 4 Vsts, 4 dc and 8 3-ch-sps.
Fasten off Mustard.

5th round: Join Duck Egg with a ss to any dc, [miss next 3-ch-sp, 9dtr in 1-ch-sp of next Vst, miss next 3-ch-sp, 1dc in next dc] to end, ss in first dtr – 40 sts.
Fasten off Duck Egg.

6th round: Join Royal with a ss to any dc, [3ch, miss next st, 1dc in next st] 4 times, 3ch, [1htr, 1ch, 1htr] in next dc; repeat from * 3 times more, ss to first of beginning 3ch – 24 sts, 20 3-ch-sps and 4 1-ch-sps.

7th round: Ss into first 3-ch-sp, 4ch (counts as 1tr, 1ch), 1tr in same 3-ch-sp, Vst in next 3-ch-sp, *[2tr, 3ch, 2tr] in next 3-ch-sp, [Vst in next 3-ch-sp] twice, Vst in next 1-ch-sp, [Vst in next 3-ch-sp] twice; repeat from * 3 times more, but on the last repeat omit the last Vst, ss to third of beginning 4ch – 5 Vsts along each side and [4tr and 3-ch-sp] in each corner.
Fasten off Royal.

8th round: Join White with a ss to any 3-ch-sp in corner, 3ch (counts as 1tr), [1tr, 3ch, 2tr] in same 3-ch-sp, 1tr in each st and in each 1-ch-sp to next 3-ch-sp, *[2tr, 3ch, 2tr] in next 3-ch-sp, 1tr in each st and in each 1-ch-sp to next 3-ch-sp; repeat from * twice more, ss to top of beginning 3ch – 92 sts and 4 3-ch-sps.
Fasten off and weave in ends.

Put it together

Join the remaining squares to the large square with the inner edging, using the chart below as a guide. Join by holding the squares with the right sides together and ss through back loops of each square to form a neat join. When joining the squares to the inner edging, use the same joining method and, where the squares join, ease the stitches so the squares are evenly spaced.

Final border

This consists of 4 rounds of border. The colours of your border can be any selection that you like. Each round of the border requires approximately 12g of yarn, so weigh your yarn before you start to ensure you have sufficient.

1st round: With 4mm hook, join Aster to any corner 3-ch-sp of the large square, *[2dc, 2ch, 2dc] in 3-ch-sp, [1ch, miss 1 st, 1dc in next st] until you reach the join of 2 squares, 1ch, 1dc in 1-ch-sp on first side of join, 1ch, 1dc in 1-ch-sp at next side of join; repeat from * 5 times more, [1ch, miss 1 st, 1dc in next st] to the last st before corner 3-ch-sp, 1ch**; repeat from * to ** until the end, ss in first dc.
Fasten off Aster.

2nd round: Join Royal to any 2-ch-sp in corner, *[2dc, 2ch, 2dc] in 2-ch-sp, 1ch, [1dc in next 1-ch-sp, 1ch] to next corner; repeat from * to end, ss to first dc.
Fasten off Royal.
Round 2 forms the pattern. Repeat once with Duck Egg and once with Mustard.
Fasten off and weave in ends.

Layout for sewing squares together

1	5	4	2	4	5	1
5	Inner Edging					5
4		1	2	1		4
2		2	1	2		2
4		1	2	1		4
5						5
1	5	4	2	4	5	1

Make for anyone blanket

This variegated yarn project creates a beautiful blanket that is perfect for everybody

Measurements

Complete blanket measures approximately 120 x 160cm (47 x 63in) when blocked. Each block measures approx 14cm (5½in) square when blocked.

Materials

For complete blanket: Variegated yarn in seven complementary colours (1 x 50g ball each). We used Sirdar Crofter DK (60% acrylic/25% cotton/15% wool, 50g/165m per ball) in: Magilly (0039), Iona (0043), Seagrass (0045), Crosbie (0041), Glendale (0038), Hepburn (0033), Hound Dog (0053). You also need 6 x 50g cream/muslin coloured yarn. We used Sirdir Calico DK (60% cotton/40% acrylic, 50g/158m per ball) in Muslin (724). 3.5mm crochet hook and tapestry needle.

Gauge

Each block measures approx. 5½in square when blocked.

Abbreviations

Ch, chain; **st(s)**, stitch(es); **dc**, double crochet; **tr**, treble crochet; **ss**, slip stitch.

To make

Variegated yarn gives a distressed look, and the bonus is that you don't need to keep changing colours (not until the very end anyway).

Everything about this pattern has been kept simple in order to show off the cool yarn effect. Because of this, the blanket hooks together very quickly. Perfect for a night in front of the tube!

Granny squares

(Make 80)

The first four rounds of the granny square are crocheted in one of the coloured, variegated yarns. The final (fifth) round of every square is crocheted in cream/ muslin (Calico). The colour layout is totally random.

Foundation: Using any of your coloured yarns, make a 4 ch foundation ch. Join into a ring with a ss.

Round 1: Ch3 (acts as first tr), 2tr, (ch2, 3tr) 3 times, ch2, join with a ss to 3rd st of the starting ch-3.

Round 2: Ch3 (acts as first tr), 2tr, *(2tr, ch2, 2tr) in ch-2 space from previous round, 3tr, repeat from * 2 times (ie, 3 times in total), (2tr, ch2, 2tr) in ch-2 space, join with a ss to 3rd st of the starting ch-3.

Round 3: Ch3 (acts as first tr), 4tr, *(2tr, ch2, 2tr) in ch-2 space from previous round, 7tr, repeat from * 2 times (so 3 times in total), (2tr, ch2, 2tr) in ch-2 space, 2tr, join with a ss to 3rd st of the starting ch-3.

Round 4: Ch3 (acts as first tr), 6tr, *(2tr, ch2, 2tr) in ch-2 space from previous round, 11tr, repeat from * 2 times (ie, 3 times in total), (2tr, ch2, 2tr) in ch-2 space, 4tr, join with a ss to 3rd st of the starting ch-3. Break yarn.

Round 5: Join cream/muslin yarn into a corner ch-2 space.

[Ch3 (acts as first tr), 1tr, ch2, 2tr] in ch-2 space, 15tr, *(2tr, ch2, 2tr) in ch-2 space from previous round, 15tr, repeat from * 2 times (3 times in total). Join with a ss to 3rd st of the starting ch-3. Break yarn.

Joining and finishing

When all 80 squares are complete, block each square. Using cream/muslin yarn, join the squares together in eight rows of 10 squares in a random order – or whichever design you like. Join them by placing the right sides of two squares together, and dc into the top of each tr of the final round. Join the eight strips together in the same way by placing the right sides of each strip together as you did the squares.

Border

Using the cream/muslin yarn, crochet a border of two rows of dc stitches around the entire blanket, working around the corners by placing 2 ch stitches at each corner. Break off. Sew in all loose ends to finish. Now give yourself a good pat on the back.

ANITA MUNDT

Anita studied textile design while she was at university in Yorkshire. Although she no longer works in the textile industry, creating with textiles is very much in her heart. She now lives in an old village school, which she is slowly renovating with her husband.

Baby blankets

Create cosy and soft blankets to keep your little one warm and snug

- [x] EASY PEASY
- [ ] A BIT MORE TRICKY
- [ ] HARD-ISH
- [ ] QUITE A CHALLENGE

Striped blanket

Super stripes for pram or buggy, or just for snuggling

To make

With 3.5mm hook and Rose, make 92ch.
Foundation row: 1dc in 2nd ch from hook (counts as 1dc), [1dc in next ch] to end, turn – 91dc.
Pattern row: 1ch (does not count as a st throughout), [1dc in next dc] to end.
Pattern another row.
Joining in and breaking off colours as required, work in stripes thus – Pattern 3 rows Aqua, 3 rows Ecru, 3 rows Lime, 3 rows Denim and 3 rows Rose.
Repeat last 15 rows, 8 times more.
Pattern 3 rows Aqua, 3 rows Ecru and 3 rows Lime. Fasten off.

Measurements

Approximately 48 x 66cm (19 x 26in), including edging.

Materials

For complete blanket: 2 x 50g (125m) balls of Debbie Bliss Eco Baby (100% cotton) in Denim (29) and 1 ball in each of Rose (12), Aqua (05), Ecru (16) and Lime (50). Size 3.5mm crochet hook.

Tension

21 stitches and 24 rows, to 10 x 10cm (4 x 4in), over double crochet, using 3.5mm hook.

Abbreviations

Ch, chain; **st(s)**, stitch(es); **dc**, double crochet; **tr**, treble.

Note

Yarn amounts are based on average requirements and are therefore approximate.
Instructions in square brackets are worked as stated after 2nd bracket.

Top edging

With wrong side facing, using 3.50 hook and Denim, work across last row worked like this –
1st row: 1ch, 2dc in first dc, [1dc in next dc] 89 times, 2dc in last dc, turn – 93dc.
2nd row: 1ch, 2dc in first dc, [1dc in next dc] 91 times, 2dc in last dc, turn – 95dc.
3rd row: 1ch, 2dc in first dc, [1dc in next dc] 93 times, 2dc in last dc, turn – 97dc.
4th row: 1ch, 1dc in first dc, [miss next 2dc, 5tr in next dc, miss next 2dc, 1dc in next dc] 16 times. Fasten off.

Side edging

(both alike)

1st row: With wrong side facing, using 3.5mm hook and Denim, work 1ch, 2dc in first row-end of side edge, then 119dc evenly along row-ends to last row-end, 2dc in last row-end, turn – 123dc.
2nd row: 1ch, 2dc in first dc, [1dc in next dc] 121 times, 2dc in last dc, turn – 125dc.
3rd row: 1ch, 2dc in first dc, [1dc in next dc] 123 times, 2dc in last dc, turn – 127dc.
4th row: 1ch, 1dc in first dc, [miss next 2dc, 5tr in next dc, miss next 2dc, 1dc in next dc] 21 times. Fasten off.

Bottom edging

1st row: With wrong side facing, using 3.5mm hook and Denim, work across base ch edge thus: 1ch, 2dc in first base ch, [1dc in next base ch] 89 times, 2dc in last base ch – 93dc.
2nd row: 1ch, 2dc in first dc, [1dc in next dc] 121 times, 2dc in last dc, turn – 125dc.
3rd row: 1ch, 2dc in first dc, [1dc in next dc] 123 times, 2dc in last dc, turn – 127dc.
4th row: 1ch, 1dc in first dc, [miss next 2dc, 5tr in next dc, miss next 2dc, 1dc in next dc] 21 times. Fasten off.

To complete

Join row-ends of edgings together at each corner.

With much love...

A soft and comforting blanket for a newborn babe

Measurements

Complete blanket measures approximately 67 x 77cm (26¼ x 30¼in).

Materials

For the set: 4 x 50g (125m) balls of Rico Design Baby Cotton Soft DK (50% cotton, 50% acrylic) in each of White (001), Lobster (029) and Mint (031). Length of black yarn for embroidery.
Size 3.5mm crochet hook.

Tension

22 stitches and 25 rows, to 10 x 10cm (4 x 4in), over double crochet, using 3.5mm hook.

Abbreviations

Ch, chain; **st(s)**, stitch(es); **dc**, double crochet; **tr**, treble; **htr**, half treble; **ss**, slip st; **ch-sp**, chain space; **yrh**, yarn round hook; **dc2tog**, work 2dc together thus: [insert hook in next st, yrh and pull through] twice, yrh and pull through all 3 loops on hook; **tr2tog**, work 2tr together thus: [yrh, insert hook in next st, yrh and pull through, yrh and pull through first 2 loops on hook] twice, yrh and pull through all 3 loops on hook.

Note

Yarn amounts are based on average requirements and are therefore approximate.
Instructions in square brackets are worked as stated after 2nd bracket.

Motif

(Make 42)

With 3.5mm hook and Mint, make 21ch.

1st row: 1dc in 2nd ch from hook (counts as 1 st), 1dc in each ch to end, turn – 20dc.

Twisting yarns together on wrong sides when changing colours and working last dc before colour change as follows: with yarn used, insert hook in next dc, yrh and pull through, with next colour, yrh and pull through 2 loops on hook, continue thus:

2nd row: With Mint, 1ch (does not count as a st throughout), 1dc in each of first 19dc, with White, 1dc in last dc, turn.

3rd row: With White, 1ch, 1dc in each of first 2dc, with Mint, 1dc in each of last 18dc, turn.

4th row: With Mint, 1ch, 1dc in each of first 17dc, with White, 1dc in each of last 3dc, turn.

5th row: With White, 1ch, 1dc in each of first 4dc, with Mint, 1dc in each of last 16dc, turn.

6th row: With Mint, 1ch, 1dc in each of first 15dc, with White, 1dc in each of last 5dc, turn.

7th row: With White, 1ch, 1dc in each of first 6dc, with Mint, 1dc in each of last 14dc, turn.

8th row: With Mint, 1ch, 1dc in each of first 13dc, with White, 1dc in each of last 7dc, turn.

9th row: With White, 1ch, 1dc in each of first 8dc, with Mint, 1dc in each of last 12dc, turn.

10th row: With Mint, 1ch, 1dc in each of first 11dc, with White, 1dc in each of last 9dc, turn.

11th row: With White, 1ch, 1dc in each of first 10dc, with Mint, 1dc in each of last 10dc, turn.

12th row: With Mint, 1ch, 1dc in each of first 9dc, with White, 1dc in each of last 11dc, turn.

13th row: With White, 1ch, 1dc in each of first 12dc, with Mint, 1dc in each of last 8dc, turn.

14th row: With Mint, 1ch, 1dc in each of first 7dc, with White, 1dc in each of last 13dc, turn.

15th row: With White, 1ch, 1dc in each of first 14dc, with Mint, 1dc in each of last 6dc, turn.

16th row: With Mint, 1ch, 1dc in each of first 5dc, with White, 1dc in each of last 15dc, turn.

17th row: With White, 1ch, 1dc in each of first 16dc, with Mint, 1dc in each of last 4dc, turn.

18th row: With Mint, 1ch, 1dc in each of first 3dc, with White, 1dc in each of last 17dc, turn.

19th row: With White, 1ch, 1dc in each of first 18dc, with Mint, 1dc in each of last 2dc, turn.

20th row: With Mint, 1ch, 1dc in first dc, with White 1dc in each of last 19dc, turn.

21st row: With White, 1ch, 1dc in each of 20dc. Fasten off.

Edging: With right side facing and using 3.5mm hook, join Lobster to first ch on base chain of motif and work 1dc in each of 20ch, 1ch for corner, 20dc along row-end edge, 1ch for corner, 1dc in each of 20dc along fastened off edge, 1ch for corner, 20dc along other row-end edge, 1ch for corner, ss in first dc.

Next round: [1dc in each dc to corner ch-sp, work 1dc, 1ch and 1dc all in corner ch-sp] 4 times, ss in first dc. Fasten off.

To make up

Arrange motifs in 6 rows of 7 motifs each. Working horizontally, place motifs with wrong sides together, using 3.5mm hook and Lobster, joining motifs by working ss into back loops of each corresponding pair of stitches. Join motifs vertically in same way.

Border: With right side facing and using 3.5mm hook, join Lobster with ss to any corner ch-sp, 3ch (counts as 1tr), *1tr in each of next 21dc, [tr2tog over next dc and ch-sp, tr2tog over next ch-sp and dc, 1dc in each of next 20dc] to last motif before corner, tr2tog over next dc and ch-sp, tr2tog over next ch-sp and dc, 1dc in each of next 21dc, work 1tr, 1ch, 1tr, 1ch and 1tr all in corner ch-sp, repeat from * 3 times more, ending with work 1tr, 1ch, 1tr and 1ch all in same ch-sp as ss, ss in top of 3ch – 592 sts.

Next 3 rounds: 3ch, [1tr in each tr to first ch-sp at corner, 1tr in ch-sp, work 1tr, 1ch, 1tr, 1ch and 1tr all in next tr, 1tr in next ch-sp] 4 times, ss in top of 3ch.
Fasten off and neaten ends.

- ☑ EASY PEASY
- ☐ A BIT MORE TRICKY
- ☐ HARD-ISH
- ☐ QUITE A CHALLENGE

Measurements

Approximately 83 x 87cm (32¾ x 34¼in).

Materials

For complete blanket: 1 x 100g (295m) ball of Stylecraft Special DK (100% acrylic) in each of Magenta (1084), Pomegranate (1083), Apricot (1026), Citron (1263), Pistachio (1822), Grass Green (1821), Duck Egg (1820), Sage (1725) and Denim (1302).
Size 4mm crochet hook; thick card for tassel making.

Tension

4 pattern repeats and 9 rows, to measure 10 x 10cm (4 x 4in), over pattern, using 4mm hook.

Abbreviations

Ch, chain; **ch-sp(s)**, chain space(s); **blo**, back loop only; **dc**, double crochet; **htr**, half treble crochet; **ss**, slip stitch; **st(s)**, stitch(es); **yrh**, yarn round hook; **4trcl**, 4 treble crochet cluster stitch thus: [yrh, insert hook into st or space as indicated, yrh and pull loop through, yrh, pull through first 2 loops only] 4 times (5 loops on hook), yrh and pull through all 5 loops.

Note

You can use yarn stash oddments to make your blanket, noting that if you use a different weight of yarn, your blanket will be a different size. Use the hook size that is recommended for your yarn. Yarn amounts are based on average requirements and are therefore approximate. Instructions in brackets are worked as stated after 2nd bracket.

Sherbet stripes

Our candy-coloured blanket is finished with tassels

Blanket stripe sequence

Stripes are worked in the following colour sequence throughout.

1 row each of:

- Magenta
- Pomegranate
- Apricot
- Citron
- Pistachio
- Grass Green
- Duck Egg
- Sage

Main blanket

With Magenta, ch152.

1st row (right side): 1dc in 2nd ch from hook, [3ch, 4trcl over next 4 ch, 1ch, 1dc in next ch] to end, changing to Pomegranate on last yrh of last dc, turn – 30 pattern repeats and 1dc.

2nd row: 3ch, [1dc in top of next 4trcl, 3ch, 4trcl in 3ch-sp, 1ch] to last st, 1dc in last st, changing to Apricot on last yrh of last dc, turn.

3rd row: 3ch, [1dc in top of next 4trcl, 3ch, 4trcl in 3ch-sp, 1ch] to last dc, skip last dc, 1dc in top of beginning 3ch from beginning of previous row changing to next colour on last yrh of last dc, turn. 3rd row forms pattern.

Repeat 3rd row, changing colour as before on last yrh of last dc of each row, following the colour sequence given, until you have finished 11 colour repeats in total. Blanket should measure approximately 75 x 79cm (29 x 31in). Fasten off on last row and weave in all ends before beginning the border.

Border

Take care to evenly space your htr sts in 1st round, to prevent blanket from warping. As a guide, this is approximately 4 htr for each pattern repeat across top and bottom, and approximately 3 htr for every 2 rows along sides. Note that specific stitch counts are not given, as your stitch count may vary depending on your tension.

1st round (right side): With Denim, and with right side facing, join yarn in top-right corner space, 2ch (counts as a 1htr), work (1htr, 2ch, 1htr) in same space, work htr evenly around the blanket edge, working (2htr, 2ch, 2htr) in each corner, ss in top of beginning 2ch, ss in next htr, ss into corner 2ch-sp.

2nd round: 1ch (this does not count as a st), work (1dc, 2ch, 1dc) in each corner and then 1dcblo in each st around the blanket edge, ss in first dc and fasten off – 8 sts increased.

When working 3rd to 7th rounds, fasten off at end of each round then start the next colour in a different corner. This gives a neater finish. If at any point your blanket edge is pulling in, work (2dc, 2ch, 2dc) in each corner on next round.

3rd to 7th rounds: Use colours in the following order: Pistachio, Citron, Apricot, Pomegranate, Magenta. Join yarn to any corner 2ch-sp with a ss, 1ch (does not count as a st), (1dc, 2ch, 1dc) in corner space, continue working 1dc in each st all around blanket edge and (1dc, 2ch, 1dc) in corner spaces, ss in first dc, fasten off – 8 sts increased.

8th round: Join Denim in any corner 2ch-sp with a ss, 2ch (counts as first htr), work (1htr, 2ch, 2htr) in corner space, continue working 1htr in each st around blanket edge and (2htr, 2ch, 2htr) in corner spaces, ss in top of beginning 2ch – 16 sts increased.

Fasten off and weave in ends.

To finish

Because you have worked several rounds of double crochet stitches, the blanket may not sit completely flat. This can be rectified by gently pulling it flat and then blocking with water.

Using all colours held together and a piece of thick card, make 4 tassels and attach one to each corner.

Hippo blanket

Crochet a cute hippo comforter for a little one to love

- ☐ EASY PEASY
- ☑ A BIT MORE TRICKY
- ☐ HARD-ISH
- ☐ QUITE A CHALLENGE

Measurements

Blanket section measures approximately 32 x 32cm (12¾ x 12¾in) when flat.

Materials

For complete blanket: 1 x 150g (480m) yarn cake of King Cole Curiosity DK (100% acrylic) in Mother of Pearl (2904). Size 3.5mm crochet hook; small amount of toy filling; 1m (39in) length of black yarn or embroidery thread for eyes.

Tension

5.5 rounds of blanket measure 10 x 10cm (4 x 4in), over treble crochet, using 3.5mm hook.

Abbreviations

Ch(s), chain(s); **ch-sp(s)**, chain space(s); **dc**, double crochet; **dc2tog**, double crochet 2 sts together (to decrease) thus: [insert hook in next st, yrh and pull through] twice, yrh and pull through all 3 loops; **ss**, slip stitch; **sp(s)**, space(s); **st(s)**, stitch(es); **tr**, treble crochet; **yrh**, yarn round hook.

Note

Yarn cake has a grey section and a pink section. Use grey section for head, arms and blanket edge, and pink section for blanket. Yarn amounts are based on average requirements and are approximate. Instructions in square brackets are worked as stated after 2nd bracket.

Hippo

Head

1st round: With 3.5mm hook and grey section of yarn, make a slip ring as follows: wind yarn round index finger of left hand to form a ring, insert hook into ring, yrh and pull through, 1ch (does not count as a st), work 6dc in ring, pull end of yarn tightly to close ring – 6 sts. Continue to work in a spiral without closing each round.
2nd round: [2dc in next st] 6 times – 12 sts.
3rd round: [1dc in next st, 2dc in next st] 6 times – 18 sts.
4th round: [1dc in next 2 sts, 2dc in next st] 6 times – 24 sts.
5th round: [1dc in next 3 sts, 2dc in next st] 6 times – 30 sts.
6th to 9th rounds: [1dc in next st] 6 times.
10th round: [1dc in next 3 sts, dc2tog] 6 times – 24 sts.
11th round: [1dc in next st] to end.
12th round (work in front loops only): 1dc in next 8 sts, 2dc in each of next 8 sts, 1dc in next 8 sts – 32 sts.
13th and 14th rounds: [1dc in next st] to end.
15th round: [1dc in next 7 sts, 2dc in next st] 4 times – 36 sts.
16th and 17th rounds: [1dc in next st] to end.
18th round: [1dc in next 7 sts, dc2tog] 4 times – 32 sts.
19th round: [1dc in next 2 sts, dc2tog] 8 times – 24 sts.
20th round: [1dc in next st] to end.
21st round: [1dc in next st, dc2tog] 8 times – 16 sts.
Fill head firmly with toy filling.
22nd round: [1dc in next st] to end.
23rd round: [Dc2tog] 8 times – 8 sts.
Ss in next st. Cut yarn and fasten off. Add a little more toy filling if needed. Gather stitches to close the hole.

Ears (both alike)

Work as for head to end of 2nd round – 12 sts.
3rd round: [1dc in next st] to end.
Ss in next st. Cut yarn and fasten off. Pinch one end of ear together and secure with a few stitches. Sew ears to each side of head, near to top.

Arms (both alike)

Work as for head to end of 2nd round – 12 sts.
3rd and 4th round: [1dc in next st] to end.
5th round: [1dc in next 2 sts, dc2tog] 3 times – 9 sts.
6th round: 1dc in next 3 sts, dc2tog, 1dc in next 2 sts, dc2tog – 7 sts.
7th to 14th rounds: [1dc in next st] to end.
Ss into next st. Cut yarn and fasten off. Fill arm with toy filling, flatten top seam and whip stitch together. Sew flat seam of each arm to base of head, leaving approx 3cm (1in) gap between them.

Blanket

1st round: With 3.5mm hook and pink section of yarn, make a slip ring as follows: wind yarn round index finger of left hand to form a ring, insert hook into ring, yrh and pull through, 3ch, (counts as first tr), work 2tr in ring, 2ch (for first corner), [3tr in ring, 2ch] 3 times, ss in top of beginning 3ch to join. Pull end of yarn tightly to close ring – 4 3tr-groups and 4 2ch-sps.
2nd round: Ss in each of next 2 tr, ss into corner 2ch-sp, 3ch (counts as first tr here and throughout), [2tr, 2ch, 3tr] in same 2ch-sp, *[3tr, 2ch, 3tr] in next 2ch-sp; repeat from * twice more, ss in top of beginning 3ch – 2 3tr-groups along each side and 4 2ch-sps.
3rd round: Ss in each of next 2 tr, ss into corner 2ch-sp, 3ch, [2tr, 2ch, 3tr] in same 2ch-sp, 3tr in next space between 3tr-groups, *[3tr, 2ch, 3tr] in next corner 2ch-sp, 3tr in next space between 3tr-groups; repeat from * twice more, ss in top of beginning 3ch – 3 3tr-groups along each side and 4 2ch-sps.
4th round: Ss in each of next 2 tr, ss into corner 2ch-sp, 3ch, [2tr, 2ch, 3tr] in same 2ch-sp, [3tr in next space between 3tr-groups] to next corner 2ch-sp, *[3tr, 2ch, 3tr] in corner ch2-sp, 3tr in next space between 3tr-groups] to next corner 2ch-sp; repeat from * twice more, ss in top of beginning 3ch – 4 3tr-groups along each side and 4 2ch-sps.
Repeat 4th round, a further 12 times – 16 3tr-groups along each side and 4 ch-sps.
Fasten off pink section of yarn.
Next round (work in back loops only): Join grey section of yarn to any corner 2ch-sp with ss, 1ch (does not count as a st here and throughout), 3dc in same corner 2ch-sp, [1dc in next st] to next corner 2ch-sp, *3dc in corner 2ch-sp, [1dc in next st] to next corner 2ch-sp; repeat from * twice more, ss in back loop only of first dc to join – 204 dc.
Next round (work in back loops only): Ss in next st (you are now at centre stitch of corner), 1ch, 3dc in same st, [1dc in next st] to next corner st, *3dc in corner st, [1dc in next st] to next corner st; repeat from * twice more, ss in back loop only of first dc to join – 212 dc.
Fasten off.

To make up

Embroider eyes with black yarn or embroidery thread, positioning them above snout, and embroider nostrils with grey section of yarn on front of snout. Sew base of head (between arms) firmly to centre of blanket.

- ☑ EASY PEASY
- ☐ A BIT MORE TRICKY
- ☐ HARD-ISH
- ☐ QUITE A CHALLENGE

Cot blanket & bumper

Sweet dreams (almost) guaranteed

Blanket

Main part: With 4mm hook, make 84ch.

Foundation row (wrong side): 1tr in 4th ch from hook (counts as 2 sts), [1tr in next ch] to end – 82 sts.

1st row: 2ch (counts as 1htr), [1fptr in each of next 8 sts, 1bptr in each of next 8 sts] to last st, 1htr in last st, turn.

2nd to 5th rows: As 1st row.

6th row: 2ch (counts as 1htr), [1bptr in each of next 8 sts, 1fptr in each of next 8 sts] to last st, 1htr in last st, turn.

7th to 10th rows: As 6th row.

These 10 rows form pattern.

Repeat these 10 rows, 5 times more, then work 1st to 5th rows again. Do not turn.

Edging: Change to 3.5mm hook.

1st round: Work along side edge of blanket thus: 2ch (counts as 1dc and 1ch), miss first row-end, [1dc in next row-end, 1ch] to end, work along ch edge thus: 1dc in first st, [1ch, miss 1 st, 1dc in next st] to last st, 1ch, miss last st, work along other side edge of blanket thus: [1dc in next row-end, 1ch] to end, work along top edge thus: 1dc in first st, [1ch, miss 1 st, 1dc in next st] to last st, 1ch, miss last st, ss in first of 2ch.

2nd and 3rd rounds: Ss in first ch-sp, 2ch (counts as 1dc and 1ch), miss 1dc, [1dc in next ch-sp, 1ch, miss 1dc] to end, ss in first of 2ch. Fasten off.

Bumper

With 4mm hook, make 196ch.

Foundation row (wrong side): 1tr in 4th ch from hook (counts as 2 sts), [1tr in next ch] to end – 194 sts.

1st row: 2ch (counts as 1htr), [1fptr in each of next 8 sts, 1bptr in each of next 8 sts] to last st, 1htr in last st, turn.

2nd to 5th rows: As 1st row.

6th row: 2ch (counts as 1htr), [1bptr in each of next 8 sts, 1fptr in each of next 8 sts] to last st, 1htr in last st, turn.

7th to 10th rows: As 6th row.

These 10 rows form pattern.

Repeat these 10 rows once more, then work 1st to 5th rows again. Do not turn.

Edging: Change to 3.5mm hook.

1st round: Work along side edge of bumper thus: 2ch (counts as 1dc and 1ch), miss first row-end, [1dc in next row-end, 1ch] to end, work along ch edge thus: 1dc in first st, [1ch, miss 1 st, 1dc in next st] to last st, 1ch, miss last st, work along other side edge of bumper thus: [1dc in next row-end, 1ch] to end, work along top edge thus: 1dc in first st, [1ch, miss 1 st, 1dc in next st] to last st, 1ch, miss last st, ss in first of 2ch.

2nd and 3rd rounds: Ss in first ch-sp, 2ch (counts as 1dc and 1ch), miss 1dc, [1dc in next ch-sp, 1ch, miss 1dc] to end, ss in first of 2ch. Fasten off.

Mark 4 tie positions on top edge of bumper: one at each end and one about 20cm from each end.

Bumper ties

(Make 4)

With 4mm hook, make 8ch.

Foundation row: 1dc in 4th ch from hook (counts as first ch-sp and 1dc), [1ch, miss 1ch, 1dc in next ch] twice, turn.

Pattern row: 2ch (counts as first ch-sp), miss first dc, [1dc in ch-sp, 1ch, miss 1dc] twice, 1dc in last ch-sp, turn.

Pattern another 30 rows.

Joining row: Place last row of tie at one marked position on top edge of bumper and work ss through every st on both layers, turn.

Next row: Work through both layers, 2ch (counts as first ch-sp), miss first st, [1dc in next st, 1ch, miss 1st] twice, 1dc in last ch-sp, turn

Pattern another 31 rows. Fasten off.

Measurements

Blanket: 44 x 52.5cm (17¼ x 20½in).

Bumper: 100 x 22.5cm (39¼ x 8¾in).

Materials

Blanket: 5 x 50g (125m) balls of Debbie Bliss Eco Baby (100% cotton) in Primrose (37).

Bumper: 5 x 50g (125m) balls of Debbie Bliss Eco Baby (100% cotton) in Primrose (37).

Both items: Size 3.5mm and 4mm crochet hooks.

Tension

16 stitches and 10 rows, to 8 x 7.5cm (3.1 x 2.9in), over pattern, using 4mm hook.

Abbreviations

Ch, chain; **dc**, double crochet; **st(s)**, stitch(es); **htr**, half treble; **tr**, treble; **fptr**, front post treble (yarn over, take hook from front to back, around post of next st then to front again, yarn over and pull through, [yarn over and pull through first 2 loops on hook] twice); **bptr**, back post treble (yarn over, take hook from back to front, around post of next st then to back again, yarn over and pull through, [yarn over and pull through first 2 loops on hook] twice); **ss**, slip st; **ch-sp**, chain space.

Note

Yarn amounts are based on average requirements and are therefore approximate. Instructions in square brackets are worked as stated after 2nd bracket.

Measurements

Approximately 70 x 100cm (27½ x 39½in).

Materials

9 x 50g (75m) balls of DMC Natura Medium (100% cotton) in White (01), 2 balls in each of Grey (12), Mint (137) and Coral (444). Size 5mm crochet hook.

Tension

22 stitches and 23 rows, to 15 x 15cm (6 x6in), over double crochet, using 5mm hook.

Abbreviations

Ch, chain; **st(s)**, stitch(es); **dc**, double crochet; **ss**, slip stitch; **yrh**, yarn round hook.

Note

Yarn amounts are based on average requirements and are therefore approximate. Instructions in square brackets are worked as stated after 2nd bracket.

- ☐ EASY PEASY
- ☑ A BIT MORE TRICKY
- ☐ HARD-ISH
- ☐ QUITE A CHALLENGE

Windmill blanket

This blanket design is cute and versatile

Motif

First square: With 5mm hook and White, make 23ch.

1st row (right side): 1dc in 2nd ch from hook (counts as 1 st), 1dc in each of next 20ch, insert hook in last ch, yrh and pull through, join in Grey, yrh and pull through 2 loops on hook, turn – 22dc.

Twisting yarns together on wrong sides when changing colours and working last dc before colour change as follows: with yarn in use, insert hook in next dc, yrh and pull through, with next colour, yrh and pull through 2 loops on hook, continue thus:

2nd row: With Grey, 1ch (does not count as a st throughout), 1dc in first dc, with White, 1dc in each of last 21dc, turn.

3rd row: With White, 1ch, 1dc in each of first 20dc, with Grey, 1dc in each of last 2dc, turn.

4th row: With Grey, 1ch, 1dc in each of first 3dc, with White, 1dc in each of last 19dc, turn.

5th row: With White, 1ch, 1dc in each of first 18dc, with Grey, 1dc in each of last 4dc, turn.

6th row: With Grey, 1ch, 1dc in each of first 5dc, with White, 1dc in each of last 17dc, turn.

7th row: With White, 1ch, 1dc in each of first 16dc, with Grey, 1dc in each of last 6dc, turn.

8th row: With Grey, 1ch, 1dc in each of first 7dc, with White, 1dc in each of last 15dc, turn.

9th row: With White, 1ch, 1dc in each of first 14dc, with Grey, 1dc in each of last 8dc, turn.

10th row: With Grey, 1ch, 1dc in each of first 9dc, with White, 1dc in each of last 13dc, turn.

11th row: With White, 1ch, 1dc in each of first 12dc, with Grey, 1dc in each of last 10dc, turn.

12th row: With Grey, 1ch, 1dc in each of first 11dc, with White, 1dc in each of last 11dc, turn.

13th row: With White, 1ch, 1dc in each of first 10dc, with Grey, 1dc in each of last 12dc, turn.

14th row: With Grey, 1ch, 1dc in each of first 13dc, with White, 1dc in each of last 9dc, turn.

15th row: With White, 1ch, 1dc in each of first 8dc, with Grey, 1dc in each of last 14dc, turn.

16th row: With Grey, 1ch, 1dc in each of first 15dc, with White, 1dc in each of last 7dc, turn.

17th row: With White, 1ch, 1dc in each of first 6dc, with Grey, 1dc in each of last 16dc, turn.

18th row: With Grey, 1ch, 1dc in each of first 17dc, with White, 1dc in each of last 5dc, turn.

19th row: With White, 1ch, 1dc in each of first 4dc, with Grey, 1dc in each of last 18dc, turn.

20th row: With Grey, 1ch, 1dc in first 19dc, with White, 1dc in each of last 3dc, turn.

21st row: With White, 1ch, 1dc in each of first 2dc, with Grey, 1dc in each of last 20dc, turn.

22nd row: With Grey, 1ch, 1dc in first 21dc, with White, 1dc in last dc, turn.

23rd row: With Grey, 1ch, 1dc in each of 22dc. Fasten off.

Second square: With right side facing, using 5mm hook and White, work 22dc along row-ends of Grey section of first square, changing to Grey on last stage of last dc. Work 2nd to 23rd rows as on first square.

Third square: With right side facing, using 5mm hook and White, work 22dc along row-ends of Grey section of second square, changing to Grey on last stage of last dc. Work 2nd to 23rd rows as on first square.

Fourth square: With right side facing, using 5mm hook and White, work 22dc along row-ends of Grey section of third square, changing to Grey on last stage of last dc. Work 2nd to 23rd rows as on first square. Oversew Grey section of fourth square to White section on first square to complete first motif.

Edging: With right side facing, using 5mm hook, join White to any corner on motif, 1ch, 3dc in same corner as join, [43dc along side edge to next corner, 3dc in corner] 3 times, 43dc along final edge, ss in first dc – 184 sts. Work 1 round in dc, working 3dc in centre dc at each corner. Fasten off.

Make another motif in colours as set. Make 2 more motifs, using Coral instead of Grey. Make 2 more motifs, using Mint instead of Grey.

To make up

Arrange motifs in 3 rows of 2 motifs each. Working horizontally and with wrong sides together, join motifs using 5mm hook and White, by working ss below loops of each corresponding pair of stitches along fastened-off edge.

Join motifs vertically in same way until the blanket is complete.

Border: With right side facing and using 5mm hook, join White to any corner on blanket, 1ch, 3dc in same corner as join, [1dc in each st to next corner, 3dc in corner] 3 times, 1dc in each st along final edge, ss in first dc. Work 3 rounds in dc, beginning each round with 1ch and working 3dc in centre dc at each corner on each round, ending each round with ss in first dc. Fasten off.

☐ EASY PEASY
☑ A BIT MORE TRICKY
☐ HARD-ISH
☐ QUITE A CHALLENGE

Lullaby baby set

This crocheted hat and cocoon duo makes a lighthearted and adorable gift for newborns

Cocoon

Worked in rounds that are joined.
With 4mm hook and Aspen, make 26ch.

1st round: 1htr in 3rd ch from hook (the missed 2ch counts as 1htr), 1htr in each ch to last ch, 3htr in last ch, rotate and work along opposite side of ch thus: 1htr in each of next 22 ch, 1htr in same ch as first htr, ss in back loop of top of missed 2ch – 50 sts.

2nd round: 2ch (does not count as a st), 1htrbl in same st at base of 2ch, 2htrbl in next st, 1htrbl in each of next 22 sts, 2htrbl in next st, 1htrbl in next st, 2htrbl in next st, 1htrbl in each of next 22 sts, 2htrbl in next st, ss in back loop of top of first htr – 54 sts.

3rd round: 2ch (does not count as a st), 1htrbl in same st at base of 2ch, 2htrbl in each of next 2 sts, 1htrbl in each of next 22 sts, 2htrbl in each of next 2 sts, 1htrbl in next st, 2htrbl in each of next 2 sts, 1htrbl in each of next 22 sts, 2htrbl in each of next 2 sts, ss in back loop of first htr – 62 sts.

4th round: 2ch (does not count as a st), 1htrbl in same st at base of 2ch, 1htrbl in next st, 2htrbl in each of next 2 sts, 1htrbl in each of next 24 sts, 2htrbl in each of next 2 sts, 1htrbl in each of next 3 sts, 2htrbl in each of next 2 sts, 1htrbl in each of next 24 sts, 2htrbl in each of next 2 sts, 1htrbl in next st, ss in back loop of first htr – 70 sts.

5th round: 2ch (does not count as a st), 1htrbl in same st at base of 2ch, 1htrbl in each of next 5 sts, 2htrbl in next st, [1htrbl in each of next 6 sts, 2htrbl in next st] 9 times – 80 sts.

6th round: 2ch (does not count as a st), 1htrbl in same st at base of 2ch, 1htrbl in each of next 6 sts, 2htrbl in next st, [1htrbl in each of next 7 sts, 2htrbl in next st] 9 times – 90 sts.

7th round: 2ch (does not count as a st), 1htrbl in same st at base of 2ch, 1htrbl in each of next 7 sts, 2htrbl in next st, [htrbl in each of next 8 sts, 2htrbl in next st] 9 times – 100 sts.

Now continue in rounds that are joined, but turn work after each round to keep side seam straight:

8th round (right side): 2ch (counts as 1htr), [1htr in next st] to end, ss in top of beginning 2ch, turn.

Repeat 8th round until work measures 45cm from beginning, ending after a right side round (with wrong side now facing, after turning).

Cuff

Continue in rounds that are joined, without turning after each round.

Next Round: 2ch (counts as 1htr), [1htrbl in next st] to end, ss in top of beginning 2ch.

Repeat last round 9 times more.

Next Round: [1 crab stitch in next st] to end, ss in first st, cut yarn and fasten off.

Measurements

Cocoon: Approx 45 x 32cm (17¾ x 12½in) when measured flat and with cuff folded.

Hat: Approx 38cm (15in) head circumference and 15cm (6in) deep.

Materials

For complete blanket: 2 x 100g (295m) balls of Stylecraft Special DK (100% acrylic) in Aspen (1422), 1 ball in Silver (1203) and small amounts of Midnight (1011) and Graphite (1063). Size 4mm and 3.5mm crochet hooks; toy filling.

Tension

15½ stitches, to 10cm (4in), over half treble crochet, using 4mm hook. Row tension is not critical.

Abbreviations

Ch, chain; **htr**, half treble crochet; **st(s)**, stitch(es); **ss**, slip st; **htrbl**, htr in back loop only; **yrh**, yarn round hook; **crab stitch** (also called reverse double crochet), insert hook into next st to the right, from front to back, with the hook pointing downwards, yrh and pull a loop through (2 loops on hook), yrh and pull through both loops on hook; **dc**, double crochet; **dc2tog**, dc 2 sts together (to decrease 1 st); **dc3tog**, dc 3 sts together (to decrease 2 sts); **fptr**, front post treble crochet (work a treble crochet around the post of next st, inserting hook from front); **bptr**, back post treble crochet (work a treble crochet around the post of the next st, inserting hook from back); **dcbl**, dc in back loop only; **dc2togbl**, dc 2 sts together through back loops (to decrease 1 st)

Note

Yarn amounts are based on average requirements and are therefore approximate. Instructions in square brackets are worked as stated after 2nd bracket.

Button Pad

Worked in rows. With 4mm hook and Silver, make 31ch.
1st row (right side): 1htr in 3rd ch from hook (the missed 2ch counts as 1 htr), [1htr in next ch] to end, turn – 30 sts.
2nd row: 2ch (counts as 1htr), [1htr in next st] to end, turn.
Repeat 2nd row 8 times more, or until button pad measures 10cm (4in). Now fasten off.
With right side facing, rejoin Silver to top-right corner, 1ch (does not count as a st), 3dc in same st, now work a dc border all around the button pad, working 3dc in each corner st. Fasten off.
Insert hook into any border st, yrh with Midnight and pull through to front, now work 1ss in every st around the button pad. Fasten off, then thread yarn on to a wool/tapestry needle and weave through first st to join the line of sts.

Play button

Worked in rows. With 4mm hook and Midnight, make 10ch.
1st row: 1dc in 2nd ch from hook, [1dc in next ch] to end, turn – 9 sts.
2nd row: 1ch (does not count as a st, here and throughout), dc2tog, 1dc in each of next 5 sts, dc2tog, turn – 7 sts.
3rd row: 1ch, [1dc in next st] to end, turn.
4th row: 1ch, dc2tog, 1dc in each of next 3 sts, dc2tog, turn – 5 sts.
5th row: 1ch, [1dc in next st] to end, turn.
6th row: 1ch, dc2tog, 1dc in next st, dc2tog, turn – 3 sts.
7th row: 1ch, [1dc in next st] to end, turn.
8th row: 1ch, dc3tog – 1 st. Do not fasten off. Next, work a ss border all around the triangle to neaten the edges. Fasten off.

Pause button

(Make 2)
Worked in rows. With 4mm hook and Midnight, make 10ch.
1st row: 1dc in 2nd ch from hook, [1dc in next ch] to end, turn – 9 sts.
2nd row: 1ch (does not count as a st), [1dc in next st] to end.
Repeat 2nd row once more. Do not fasten off. Next, work a ss border all around the rectangle to neaten the edges. Cut yarn and fasten off.
Sew the play and pause buttons to the button pad, using the photo as a guide.
Pin and sew the button pad to the front of cocoon, a few rounds below the folded cuff.

Music note

NOTE STEMS (make 3)
Worked in rows. With 4mm hook and Midnight, make 17ch.

1st row: 1dc in 2nd ch from hook, [1dc in next ch] to end, turn – 16 sts.
2nd row: 1ch (does not count as a st here and throughout), [1dc in next st] to end, turn.
Repeat 2nd row once more.
4th row: 1ch, 1dc in each of next 3 sts, turn and work on these 3 sts only.
5th-15th rows: 1ch, [1dc in next st] to end, turn.
Fasten off.
With wrong side facing, count 3 sts in from the left-hand side of 3rd row and rejoin yarn to this st.
Next row: 1ch, 1dc in same st, 1dc in each of next 2 sts, turn – 3 sts.
Next row: 1ch, [1dc in next st] to end, turn.
Repeat last row 12 more times.
Do not fasten off. Work a ss border on right side, all around the shape to neaten the edges. Fasten off.

Note heads

(Make 2)
Worked in a continuous spiral without joining rounds. With 4mm hook and Midnight, make 2ch.
1st round: 6dc in 2nd ch from hook – 6 sts.
2nd round: [2dc in next st] 6 times – 12 sts.
3rd round: [1dc in next st, 2dc in next st] 6 times – 18 sts.
4th round: [1ss in next st] to end. Fasten off.
Sew stems to the front of cocoon, a few rounds below the folded cuff, using the photo as a guide. Sew the note head to the stems and position them to make one stem appear slightly longer than the other.

Hat

Worked in a continuous spiral without joining rounds.
With 4mm hook and Silver, make a slip ring as follows: wind yarn round index finger of left hand to form a ring, insert hook into ring, yarn over hook and pull through, 1ch, work 1st round in ring, then pull end of yarn tightly to close ring.
1st round: 10htr in magic loop – 10 sts.
2nd round: [2htrbl in next st] to end – 20 sts.
3rd round: [1htrbl in next st, 2htrbl in next st] 10 times – 30 sts.
4th round: [1htrbl in each of next 2 sts, 2htrbl in next st] 10 times – 40 sts.
5th round: [1htrbl in each of next 3 sts, 2htrbl in next st] 10 times – 50 sts.
6th round: [1htrbl in each of next 4 sts, 2htrbl in next st] 10 times – 60 sts.
7th round: [1htrbl in each of next 5 sts, 2htrbl in next st] 10 times – 70 sts.
8th-16th rounds: [1htrbl in next st] to end.
At the end of last round, join with a ss around post of next st.
Change to 3.5mm hook.
1st rib round: 3ch (counts as first fptr), 1bptr in next st, [1fptr in next st, 1bptr in next st] to end, ss around post of beg 3ch.
Repeat 1st rib round 4 times more.
Fasten off.

Headphones

Headband
With 4mm hook and Graphite, make 6ch.
1st row (right side): 1dc in 2nd ch from hook, [1dc in next ch] to end, turn – 5 sts.
2nd row: 1ch (does not count as a st), [1dc in next st] to end, turn.
Repeat 2nd row until headband fits over the hat, from ear to ear, ending with right side facing. Do not fasten off. Next, work a ss border on right side, all around the shape to neaten the edges. Fasten off.

Ear pads

Worked in a continuous spiral in back loops, without joining rounds. With 4mm hook and Graphite, make 2ch.
1st round: 6dc in 2nd ch from hook – 6 sts.
2nd round: [2dcbl in next st] 6 times – 12 sts.
3rd round: [1dcbl in next st, 2dcbl in next st] 6 times – 18 sts.
4th round: [1dcbl in next st, 2dcbl in next st] 9 times – 27 sts.
5th round: [1dcbl in each of next 2 sts, 2dcbl in next st] 9 times – 36 sts.
6th round: [1dcbl in each of next 3 sts, 2dcbl in next st] 9 times – 45 sts.
7th round: [1dcbl in each st] to end.
8th round: [1dcbl in each of next 3 sts, dc2togbl] 9 times – 36 sts.
9th round: [1dcbl in each of next 2 sts, dc2togbl] 9 times – 27 sts. Fasten off.

To make up

Sew headband in place on hat, using photo as a guide. Fill each ear pad lightly with toy filling to create a disc shape (which is slightly more flat than rounded). Sew ear pads in place on each side of hat at base of headband.

- [x] EASY PEASY
- [ ] A BIT MORE TRICKY
- [ ] HARD-ISH
- [ ] QUITE A CHALLENGE

Granny squares baby blanket

Put a new spin on the traditional square by combining different sizes in a patchwork baby blanket

Measurements

Complete blanket measures approximately 60 x 60cm (23.6 x 23.6in).

Materials

For complete blanket: 2 x 50g (95m) balls of Sirdar Snuggly Baby Bamboo DK (80% bamboo, 20% wool) in each of Hush a Bye (109), Putty (132), Cream (131) and Bobby Blue (115).
Size 4mm crochet hook.

Tension

Large square measures 12 x 12cm (4.7 x 4.7in) square on 4mm hook.

Abbreviations

ch, chain; **st(s)**, stitch(es); **ss**, slip stitch; **tr**, treble; **ch-sp**, space. are worked as stated after 2nd bracket.

To make

Small square (make 48)

Using Cream, make slip ring.

1st round: 3ch (counts as 1tr), 2tr in ring, 2ch, [3tr in ring, 2ch] 3 times, ss in top of 3ch – 4 groups of 3tr. Fasten off.

2nd round: Join Putty in next corner ch-sp, 3ch, (2tr, 2ch, 3tr) in same ch-sp, *1ch, (3tr, 2ch, 3tr) in next ch-sp; repeat from * twice more, 1ch, ss in top of 3ch. Fasten off.

3rd round: Join Hush a Bye in next corner ch-sp, 3ch, (2tr, 2ch, 3tr) in same ch-sp, *1ch, 3tr in next ch-sp, 1ch, (3tr, 2ch, 3tr) in corner ch-sp; repeat from * twice more, 1ch, 3tr in next ch-sp, 1ch, ss in top of 3ch. Fasten off. Make 11 more in the same colourway. Make 36 more small squares as follows:

Make 12: 1st round Putty; 2nd round Hush a Bye; 3rd round Bobby Blue.

Make 12: 1st round Hush a Bye; 2nd round Bobby Blue; 3rd round Cream.

Make 12: 1st round Bobby Blue; 2nd round Cream; 3rd round Putty.

Large square

(make 13)

Using Cream, make slip ring.

1st round: 3ch (counts as 1tr), 2tr in ring, 2ch, [3tr in ring, 2ch] 3 times, ss in top of 3ch – 4 groups of 3tr.

2nd round: Ss in each of next 2tr, ss in ch-sp, 3ch, (2tr, 2ch, 3tr) in same ch-sp, *1ch, (3tr, 2ch, 3tr) in next ch-sp; repeat from * twice more, 1ch, ss in top of 3ch. Fasten off.

3rd round: Join in Putty in next corner ch-sp, 3ch, (2tr, 2ch, 3tr) in same ch-sp, *1ch, 3tr in next ch-sp, 1ch, (3tr, 2ch, 3tr) in corner ch-sp; repeat from * twice more, 1ch, 3tr in next ch-sp, 1ch, ss in top of 3ch.

4th round: Ss in each of next 2tr, ss in ch-sp, 3ch, (2tr, 2ch, 3tr) in same ch-sp, *[1ch, 3tr in next ch-sp] twice, 1ch, (3tr, 2ch, 3tr) in next ch-sp; repeat from * twice more, [1ch, 3tr in next ch-sp] twice, 1ch, ss in top of 3ch. Fasten off.

5th round: Join Hush a Bye in next corner ch-sp, 3ch, (2tr, 2ch, 3tr) in same ch-sp, *[1ch, 3tr in next ch-sp] 3 times, 1ch, (3tr, 2ch, 3tr) in next ch-sp; repeat from * twice more, [1ch, 3tr in next ch-sp] 3 times, 1ch, ss in top of 3ch. Fasten off.

6th round: Join Bobby Blue in next corner ch-sp, 3ch, (2tr, 2ch, 3tr) in same ch-sp, *[1ch, 3tr in next ch-sp] 4 times, 1ch, (3tr, 2ch, 3tr) in next ch-sp; repeat from * twice more, [1ch, 3tr in next ch-sp] 4 times, 1ch, ss in top of 3ch. Fasten off.

To make up

Take four small squares, one of each colourway, and sew together to form a bigger square – you should have 12 in all. Lay out the blanket 5 squares by 5 squares, with a large square in each corner, and alternating large squares with set of 4 squares. Sew together.

- [ ] EASY PEASY
- [x] A BIT MORE TRICKY
- [ ] HARD-ISH
- [ ] QUITE A CHALLENGE

Lamb lovey

Create this cute and cuddly security blanket, the perfect gift for any baby

To make

Star-shaped lovey

Using col 1, make a magic ring.

Rnd 1 (RS): Work 10 dc into the ring (10 sts).

Rnd 2: ([1 dc and 1 tr3cl] in next st) 10 times, ss into 1st st (20 sts).

Rnd 3: (1 dc in next st, Corner 1 in next st, 1 dc in next st, sk next st) 5 times, ss into 1st st (30 sts).

Rnd 4: (1 dc in next st, Corner 2 in next st, 1 dc in next st, dec) 5 times (45 sts).

Rnd 5: (1 dc in next st, mbo in next st, 1 dc in next st, Corner 1 in next st, 1 dc in next st, mbo in next st, 1 dc in next st, sk next st) 5 times, ss into 1st st (50 sts).

Rnd 6: (1 dc in next 3 sts, Corner 2 in next st, 1 dc in next 3 sts, dec) 5 times (65 sts).

Rnd 7: ([1 dc in next st, mbo in next st] twice, 1 dc in next st, Corner 1 in next st, 1 dc in next st, [mbo in next st, 1 dc in next st] twice, sk 1 st) 5 times, ss in 1st st (70 sts).

Rnd 8: (1 dc in next 5 sts, Corner 2 in

Measurements

Complete blanket measures approximately 55cm (21¾in) diameter.

Materials

DK yarn in your chosen colour. We used 100g (250m) balls of acrulic yarn in: colour 1: white (3 balls) colour 2: grey (1 ball).

4.5mm hook, yarn needle, toy stuffing, pair of 10mm black safety eyes.

Tension

16 sts x 16 rows to measure 10 x 10cm (4 x 4in), using 4.5mm hook.

Abbreviations

Ch, chain; **dc**, double crochet; **st(s)**, stitch(es); **tr**, treble crochet; **yrh**, yarn round hook; **sk**, skip; **ss**, slip stitch; **sp**, space; **RS**, right side

bo, Bobble Stitch: *Yrh, insert hook into stitch or space indicated, yrh and pull a loop through so you have 3 loops on your hook. Yrh and pull through 2 loops. Repeat from * 4 more times in the same st or sp, until you have 6 loops on your hook. Yrh and pull through all 6 loops.

mbo, Modified Bobble Stitch: Similar to bo but uses 4 unfinished tr sts in the same st (so there are 5 loops on your hook before the final yrh).

tr3cl, Three Treble Crochet Cluster: 3 tr sts in the same st/sp.

Dec, decrease. Work a dc2tog as follows: insert hook in first st, yrh and pull a loop through, insert hook in next st, yrh and pull a loop through, yrh and pull through all 3 loops.

Corner 1: (**1 tr, ch 2, 1 tr**) in the same stitch (for round 3) or chain space (for rest of rounds).

Corner 2: (**2 dc, ch 2, 2 dc**) in the same chain space.

Note

In each round, the corner chains are included in the stitch count. You only join the round on rnd 2 and following alternate rounds.should tuck under their arms, and make sure they are placed with their feet at the end of their crib, Moses basket, pram etc.

next st, 1 dc in next 5 sts, dec) 5 times (85 sts).
Rnd 9: ([1 dc in next st, mbo in next st] 3 times, 1 dc in next st, Corner 1 in next st, 1 dc in next st, [mbo in next st, 1 dc in next st] 3 times, sk 1 st) 5 times, ss into 1st st (90 sts).
Rnd 10: (1 dc into next 7 sts, Corner 2 in next st, 1 dc in next 7 sts, dec) 5 times (105 sts).
Rnd 11: ([1 dc in next st, mbo in next st] 4 times, 1 dc in next st, Corner 1 in next st, 1 dc in next st, [mbo in next st, 1 dc in next st] 4 times, sk 1 st) 5 times, ss into 1st st (110 sts).
Rnd 12: (1 dc in next 9 sts, Corner 2 in next st, 1 dc in next 9 sts, dec) 5 times (125 sts).
Rnd 13: ([1 dc in next st, mbo in next st] 5 times, 1 dc in next st, Corner 1 in next st, 1 dc in next st, [mbo in next st, 1 dc in next st] 5 times, sk 1 st) 5 times, ss into 1st st 130 sts).
Rnd 14: (1 dc in next 11 sts, Corner 2 in next st, 1 dc in next 11 sts, dec) 5 times (145 sts).
Rnd 15: ([1 dc in next st, mbo in next st] 6 times, 1 dc in next st, Corner 1 in next st, 1 dc in next st, [mbo in next st, 1 dc in next st] 6 times, sk 1 st) 5 times, ss into 1st st (150 sts).
Rnd 16: (1 dc in next 13 sts, Corner 2 in next st, 1 dc in next 13 sts, dec) 5 times (165 sts).
Rnd 17: ([1 dc in next st, mbo in next st] 7 times, 1 dc in next st, Corner 1 in next st, 1 dc in next st, [mbo in next st, 1 dc in next st] 7 times, sk 1 st) 5 times, ss into 1st st (170 sts).
Rnd 18: (1 dc in next 15 sts, Corner 2 in next st, 1 dc in next 15 sts, dec) 5 times (185 sts).
Rnd 19: ([1 dc in next st, mbo in next st] 8 times, 1 dc in next st, Corner 1 in next st, 1 dc in next st, [mbo in next st, 1 dc in next st] 8 times, sk 1 st) 5 times, ss into 1st st (190 sts).
Rnd 20: (1 dc in next 17 sts, Corner 2 in next st, 1 dc in next 17 sts, dec) 5 times (205 sts).
Rnd 21: ([1 dc in next st, mbo in next st] 9 times, 1 dc in next st, Corner 1 in next st, 1 dc in next st, [mbo in next st, 1 dc in next st] 9 times, sk 1 st) 5 times, ss into next st (210 sts).
Rnd 22: (1 dc in next 19 sts, Corner 2 in next st, 1 dc in next 19 sts, dec) 5 times (225 sts).
Rnd 23: ([1 dc in next st, mbo in next st] 10 times, 1 dc in next st, Corner 1 in next

6
3
2

st, 1 dc in next st, [mbo in next st, 1 dc in next st] 10 times, sk 1 st) 5 times, ss into 1st st (230 sts).
Rnd 24: (1 dc in next 21 sts, Corner 2 in next st, 1 dc in next 21 sts, dec) 5 times (245 sts).
Rnd 25: ([1 dc in next st, mbo in next st] 11 times, 1 dc in next st, Corner 1 in next st, 1 dc in next st, [mbo in next st, 1 dc in next st] 11 times, sk 1 st) 5 times, ss into 1st st (250 sts).
Rnd 26: (1 dc in next 23 sts, Corner 2 in next st, 1 dc in next 23 sts, dec) 5 times (265 sts).
Rnd 27: ([1 dc in next st, mbo in next st] 12 times, 1 dc in next st, Corner 1 in next st, 1 dc in next st, [mbo in next st, 1 dc in next st] 12 times, sk 1 st) 5 times, ss into 1st st (270 sts).
Rnd 28: (1 dc in next 25 sts, Corner 2 in next st, 1 dc in next 25 sts, dec) 5 times (285 sts).
Rnd 29: ([1 dc in next st, mbo in next st] 13 times, 1 dc in next st, Corner 1 in next st, 1 dc in next st, [mbo in next st, 1 dc in next st] 13 times, sk 1 st) 5 times, ss into 1st st (290 sts).
Change to col 2.
Rnd 30: (1 dc in next 27 sts, Corner 2 in next st, 1 dc in next 27 sts, dec) 5 times (305 sts.)
Rnd 31: (1 dc in next 29 sts, Corner 2 in next st, 1 dc in next 29 sts, sk 1 st) 5 times (320 sts).
Finish off and weave in ends.

Head

Using col 2, make a magic ring.
Rnd 1(RS): Work 6 dc into the ring (6 sts)
Rnd 2: 2 dc in each st (12 sts).
Rnd 3: (2 dc in next st, 1 dc in next st) 6 time (18 sts).
Rnd 4: (2 dc in next st, 1 dc in next 2 sts) 6 times (24 sts).
Rnds 5-6: 1 dc in each st (24 sts).
Rnd 7: (2 dc in next st, 1 dc in next 3 sts) 6 times (30 sts).
Rnds 8-9: 1 dc in each st (30 sts).
Rnd 10: (2 dc in next st, 1 dc in next 4 sts) 6 times (36 sts).
Rnds 11-12: 1 dc in each st (36 sts).
Change to col 1.
Rnd 13: 1 dc in each st (36 sts).
Rnd 14: (1 dc in next st, 1 bo in next st) to end (36 sts).
Rnd 15: (2 dc in next st, 1 dc in next 3 sts) 9 times (45 sts).
Rnd 16: (1 dc in next st, 1 bo in next st) to last st, 1 dc in last st (45 sts).
Rnd 17: 1 dc in each st (45 sts).
Rnd 18: 1 bo in next st, (1 dc in next st, 1 bo in next st) to end (45 sts).
Rnd 19: 1 dc in each st (45 sts).
Rnd 20: 1 bo in next st, (1 dc in next st, 1 bo in next st) to end (45 sts).
Rnd 21: (Dec, 1 dc in next 3 sts) 9 times (36 sts).
Place the eyes 10 stitches apart, between rnds 10 and 11. Start filling the head with stuffing and continue stuffing as you work.
Rnd 22: (1 dc in next st, 1 bo in next st) to end (36 sts).
Rnd 23: (Dec, 1 dc in next 2 sts) 9 times (27 sts).
Rnd 24: 1 bo in next st, (1 dc in next st, 1 bo in next st) to end (27 sts).
Rnd 25: (Dec, 1 dc in next st) 9 times (18 sts).
Rnd 26: (1 dc in next st, 1 bo in next st) to end (18 sts).
Rnd 27: (Dec, 1 dc in next st) 6 times (12 sts).
Rnd 28: (1 dc in next st, 1 bo in next st) 6 times (12 sts).
Fasten off and finish filling up the head. Cut the yarn leaving a long tail, and use it to close up the hole in the head.

Ears

(Make 2)
Using col 2, make a magic ring.
Rnd 1: Work 6 dc into the ring (6 sts).
Rnd 2: 2 dc in each st (12 sts).
Rnd 3: (2 dc in next st, 1 dc in next st) 6 times(18 sts).
Rnds 4-8: 1 dc in each st (18 sts).
Rnd 9: (Dec, 1 dc in next st) 6 times. (12 sts).
Rnds 10-12: 1 dc in each st (12 sts).
Flatten ear and ss through both layers. Finish off, leaving a long tail for sewing.

Legs

(Make 2)
Using col 2, make a magic ring.
Rnd 1: Work 6 dc into the ring (6 sts).
Rnd 2: 2 dc in each st (12 sts).
Rnd 3: (2 dc in next st, 1 dc in next st) 6 times (18 sts).
Rnd 4: (2 dc in next st, 1 dc in next 5 sts) 3 times (21 sts).
Rnds 5-9: 1 dc in each st (21 sts).
Change to col 1.
Rnd 10: 1 dc in each st (21 sts).
Rnd 11: 1 dc in next 19 sts, dec. (20 sts).
Rnd 12: 1 dc in each st (20 sts).
Rnd 13: 1 dc in next 9 sts, dec, 1 dc in next 9 sts (19 sts).
Rnd 14: 1 dc in each st (19 sts).
Rnd 15: 1 dc in next 17 sts, dec (18 sts).
Rnd 16: 1 dc in each st (18 sts).
Start stuffing the leg with stuffing. Continue stuffing as you work.
Rnd 17: 1 dc in next 8 sts, dec, 1 dc in next 8 sts (17 sts).
Rnd 18: 1 dc in each st (17 sts).
Rnd 19: 1 dc in next 15 sts, dec. (16 sts).
Rnd 20: 1 dc in each st (16 sts).
Rnd 21: 1 dc in next 7 sts, dec, 1 dc in next 7 sts (15 sts).
Rnd 22: 1 dc in each st (15 sts).
Rnd 23: 1 dc in next 13 sts, dec (14 sts).
Rnd 24: 1 dc in each st (14 sts).
Finish filling leg, flatten edge and ss through both layers. Finish off, leaving a long tail for sewing.

Assembly

1 Fold each ear in half and sew a couple of stitches through the base, then sew them onto the head.
2 Sew the head in the centre of the star.
3 The two arms are attached to the star on either side of the head.

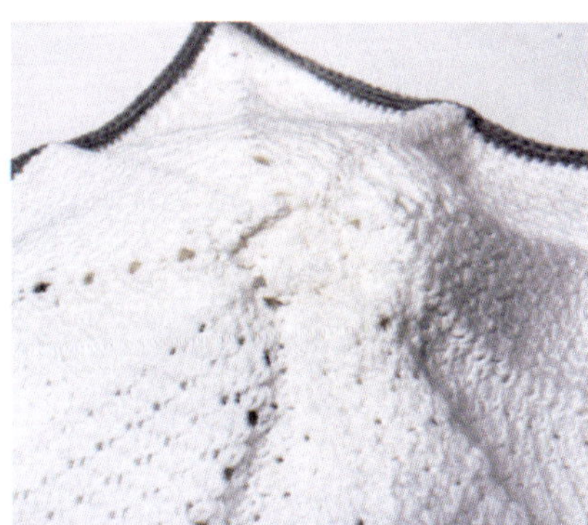

ARIANA WIMSETT

Ariana is the crochet designer behind Crafting Happiness. She specialises in nursery decor, blankets and amigurumi toys, and her patterns are fun and easy to make, designed with the beginner crocheter in mind.
craftinghappiness.com
www.facebook.com/CraftingHappinessCrochet
www.ravelry.com/designers/crafting-happiness

- ☐ EASY PEASY
- ☐ A BIT MORE TRICKY
- ☑ HARD-ISH
- ☐ QUITE A CHALLENGE

Squares baby blanket

A comfy creation to keep your little one warm and cosy

Square 1

Granny in the middle

(Make 12 squares – 1 in each of the 12 colour combinations, see pattern notes)
Using MC, make 4 ch and join with ss to form a ring.

Rnd 1 (MC): Ch 3 (counts as 1 tr), 2 tr into ring, ch 2, (3 tr into ring, ch 2) 3 times, join with ss in third ch of ch 3. Fasten off.

Rnd 2 (CC1): Join CC1 in any corner ch 2 sp. Ch 3 (counts as 1 tr), (2 tr, ch 2, 3 tr) into same ch 2 sp, *ch 1, (3 tr, ch 2, 3 tr) into next ch 2 sp; rep from * twice more, ch 1, join with ss in third ch of ch 3. Fasten off.

Rnd 3 (CC2): Join CC2 in any corner ch 2 sp. Ch 3 (counts as 1 tr), (2 tr, ch 2, 3 tr) into same ch 2 sp, *ch 1, 3 tr into next ch 1 sp, ch 1, (3 tr, ch 2, 3 tr) into next corner ch 2 sp; rep from * twice more, 3 tr into next edge ch sp, ch 1, join with ss in third ch of ch 3. Do not fasten off.

Rnd 4 (CC2): Ss into each of next 2 tr and into next corner ch 2 sp. Ch 3 (counts as 1 tr), (2 tr, ch 2, 3 tr) into same ch 2 sp, *(ch 1, 3 tr into next ch 1 sp) twice, ch 1, (3 tr, ch 2, 3 tr) into next corner ch 2 sp; rep from * twice more, (ch 1, 3 tr into next ch 1 sp) twice, ch 1, join with ss in third ch of ch 3. Fasten off.

Rnd 5 (MC): Join MC in any corner ch 2 sp. Ch 3 (counts as 1 tr), (1 tr, ch 2, 2 tr) into same ch 2 sp, *(1 tr into each of next 3 tr, 1 tr into next ch 1 sp) 3 times, 1 tr into each of next 3 tr, (2 tr, ch 2, 2 tr) into corner ch 2 sp; rep from * twice more, (1 tr into each of next 3 tr, 1 tr into next ch 1 sp) 3 times, 1 tr into each of next 3 tr, join with ss into third ch of ch 3. Do not fasten off.

Rnd 6 (MC): Ch 1 (does not count as st), 1 dc into each tr of prev round, working 5 dc into each corner ch 2 sp, join with ss into first dc. Do not fasten off.

Rnd 7 (MC): Ch 1 (does not count as st), 1 dc into each dc of prev round, working 3 dc into centre of 5 dc corner group, join with ss into first dc. Fasten off.

Square 2

Circle in a square

(Make 12 squares – 1 in each of the 12 colour combinations)
Using MC, work 4 ch and join with ss to form a ring.

Rnd 1 (MC): Ch 3 (counts as 1 tr), 15 tr into ring, join with ss into third ch of ch 3. Fasten off.

Rnd 2 (CC1): Join CC1 in sp between any 2 tr. Ch 3 (counts as 1 tr), 1 tr into same

Measurements

Complete blanket measures approx 80cm x 80cm (31½in x 31½in).

Materials

You will need to use DK weight yarn, in your chosen colours. Here we have used Sublime Baby Cashmere Merino Silk DK in: MC (main colour): Pebble, 006 (400g). CC (contrast colours): Colour 1: Vanilla 003 (100g), Colour 2: Bounty Blue 493 (100g), Colour 3: Little Lobby 494 (100g), Colour 4: Pip 381 (100g).
4mm hook.
Yarn needle.

Tension

One square to measure 12 x 12cm (4¾ x 4¾in) using 4mm crochet hook, or size required to obtain correct tension.

Abbreviations

Ch, chain; **st(s)**, stitch(es); **dc**, double crochet; **tr**, treble crochet; **ch-sp**, chain space; **sp**, space; **yrh**, yarn round hook; **ss**, slip stitch; **rev dc**, reverse double crochet; **dtr**, double treble crochet.

Special stitches

Crab stitch/reverse dc: Yrh and draw up a loop, making sure your hook faces left as it would usually. Complete the stitch as normal and then continue to work backwards along your edge. Make sure not to twist your hook!

Note

Weaving in the ends as you complete each square will make piecing your blanket together much quicker. Blocking makes a huge difference to the finish and handle of the blanket.

There are 12 colour combinations for each square: Rounds 1, 5, 6 and 7 are always worked with MC. For the feature rounds use the following combinations:

	CC1	CC2
1:	Colour 1	Colour 2
2:	Colour 1	Colour 3
3:	Colour 1	Colour 4
4:	Colour 2	Colour 1
5:	Colour 2	Colour 3
6:	Colour 2	Colour 4
7:	Colour 3	Colour 1
8:	Colour 3	Colour 2
9:	Colour 3	Colour 4
10:	Colour 4	Colour 1
11:	Colour 4	Colour 2
12:	Colour 4	Colour 3

sp, 2 tr into sp between each rem tr of prev round, join with ss into third ch of ch 3. Fasten off.

Rnd 3 (CC2): Change to CC2. Ch 3 (counts as 1 tr), 1 tr into same place, 1 tr into next tr, (2 tr into next tr, 1 tr into next tr) 15 times, join with ss into third ch of ch 3. Do not fasten off.

Rnd 4 (CC2): Ch 4 (counts as 1 dtr), (2 tr, ch 2, 2 tr, 1 dtr) into same tr, *miss 1 tr, 1 htr into each of next 3 tr, 1 dc into each of next 3 tr, 1 htr into each of next 3 tr, miss next tr, (1 dtr, 2 tr, ch 2, 2 tr, 1 dtr) into next tr; rep from * twice more, miss 1 tr, 1 htr into each of next 3 tr, 1 dc into each of next 3 tr, 1 htr into each of next 3 tr, miss next tr, join with ss into fourth ch of ch 4. Fasten off.

Rnd 5 (MC): Join MC into any corner ch 2 sp. Ch 3 (counts as 1 tr), (1 tr, ch 2, 2 tr) into same sp, *1 tr into each of next 15 sts, (2 tr, ch 2, 2 tr) into corner ch 2 sp; rep from * twice more, 1 tr into each of next 15 sts, join with ss into third ch of ch 3. Do not fasten off.

Rnd 6 (MC): Ch 1 (does not count as st), 1 dc into each tr of prev round, working 5 dc into each corner ch 2 sp, join with ss into first dc.

Rnd 7 (MC): Ch 1 (does not count as st), 1 dc into each dc of prev round, working 3 dc into centre of 5 dc corner group, join with ss into first dc. Fasten off.

Square 3

Solid square

(Make 12 squares – 1 in each of the 12 colour combinations)

Using MC, work 4 ch and join with ss to form a ring.

Rnd 1 (MC): Ch 3 (counts as 1 tr), 2 tr into ring, ch 2, (3 tr into ring, ch 2) 3 times, join with ss into third ch of ch 3. Fasten off.

Rnd 2 (CC1): Join CC1 in any corner ch 2 sp. Ch 3 (counts as 1 tr), (1 tr, ch 2, 2 tr) into same ch 2 sp, *1 tr into each of next 3 tr, (2 tr, ch 2, 2 tr) into next ch 2 sp; rep from * twice more, 1 tr into each of next 3 tr, join with ss into third ch of ch 3, do not fasten off.

Rnd 3 (CC1): Ss into next tr and into next corner ch 2 sp, ch 3 (counts as 1 tr), (1 tr, ch 2, 2 tr) into same ch 2 sp, *1 tr into each of next 7 tr, (2 tr, ch 2, 2 tr) into next ch 2 sp; rep from * twice more, 1 tr into each of next 7 tr, join with ss into third ch of ch 3. Fasten off.

Rnd 4 (CC2): Join CC2 in any corner ch 2 sp, ch 3 (counts as 1 tr), (1 tr, ch 2, 2 tr) into same ch 2 sp, *1 tr into each of next 11 tr, (2 tr, ch 2, 2 tr) into next ch 2 sp; rep from * twice more, 1 tr into each of next 11 tr, join with ss into third ch of ch 3, fasten off.

Rnd 5 (MC): Join MC in any corner ch 2 sp, ch 3 (counts as 1 tr), (1 tr, ch 2, 2 tr) into same ch 2 sp, *1 tr into each of next 15 tr, (2 tr, ch 2, 2 tr) into next ch 2 sp; rep from * twice more, 1 tr into each of next 15 tr, join with ss into third ch of ch 3. Fasten off.

Rnd 6 (MC): Ch 1 (does not count as st), 1 dc into each tr of prev round, working 5 dc into each corner ch 2 sp, join with ss into first dc.

Rnd 7 (MC): Ch 1 (does not count as st), 1 dc into each dc of prev round, working 3 dc into centre of 5 dc corner group, join with ss into first dc. Fasten off.

Making up

Weave in all loose ends. Place the squares in 6 rows of 6 squares each, moving the order about until you are pleased with the layout. Make a note of this layout so that you can refer to this as you assemble the blanket. Using MC and the flat slip-stitched seam technique, join the squares into strips of 6, then join these 6 strips together to form the blanket.

Border

With RS facing, join MC in any edge dc.

Rnd 1: Ch 1 (does not count as st), 1 dc into each dc around edge, working 3 dc into centre st of 3 dc at each corner, join with ss into first dc.

Rnds 2-3: Rep Round 1.

Rnd 4: Crab stitch edging – ch 1 (does not count as st), 1 rev dc into each dc around edge, working 3 rev dc into each corner, join with ss into first rev dc. Fasten off.

Finishing

Weave in all ends and block.

DONNA JONES
Donna designs, edits and teaches yarn crafts. She believes creative expression is essential for our wellbeing and aims to instil this in others. Follow her on Instagram
@djonesdesigns
www.donnajonesdesigns.co.uk

- ☐ EASY PEASY
- ☑ A BIT MORE TRICKY
- ☐ HARD-ISH
- ☐ QUITE A CHALLENGE

Hushabye sleeping bag

Worked in trebles with dc and a shell-edged border in a colourful palette, this granny square blanket would make a stunning on-trend addition for your home

To make

Front

Using 4mm hook and col 1, ch 55.

Row 1 (RS): 3 tr in 7th ch from hook, *miss 2 ch, 3 tr in next ch; rep from * to last 3 ch, miss 2 ch, tr in last st, turn. Place a marker at the end of this row to mark fold line. (16 treble clusters and 2 edge sts).

Row 2: Ch 3 (counts as 1st tr), 1 tr in ch-sp before next treble cluster, *3 tr in each space between treble clusters along the row to last ch-sp, 2 tr in last ch-sp, turn. (15 treble clusters with 2 half clusters).

Row 3: Ch 3 (counts as 1st tr), 3 tr in each space between treble clusters along the

Measurements

Sleeping bag measures 37 x 44cm (14.5 x 17in) excluding hood. Hood measures approx 23cm (9in) from top of bag to point.

Materials

You will need DK weight yarn in your chosen colours. We have used, Sublime Baby Cashmere Merino Silk DK in: Colour 1: Pebble 006 (250g)
Colour 2: Vanilla 003 (100g)
Colour 3: Splash 124 (50g).
4mm hook, 10 x 2.5cm (1in) buttons.

Tension

Tension is not critical for this project, but if you do not match it, your sleeping bag will vary in size to that stated and you may need more yarn. 5 pattern repeats and 11 rows measure 10cm (4in) square, using 4mm hook.

Abbreviations

Ch, chain; **st(s)**, stitch(es); **dc**, double crochet; **tr**, treble crochet; **ch-sp**, chain space; **sp**, space; **yrh**, yarn round hook; **ss**, slip stitch; **RS**, right side; **WS**, wrong side; **rdc**, reverse double crochet.

Special stitches

Crab stitch/reverse dc: Yrh and draw up a loop, making sure your hook faces left as it would usually. Complete the stitch as normal and then continue to work backwards along your edge. Make sure not to twist your hook!

Note

This project is sized for a newborn baby. It is simple to adjust the size, though. To adjust the width, add sts to the foundation chain in multiples of 3; to adjust length add rows. You'll need more yarn to make a bigger bag.

For baby's safety it is important to ensure the bag is not so large that they slip down too far as this can cause them to get overheated. As with any bedding, their face should remain above the cover, which should tuck under their arms, and make sure they are placed with their feet at the end of their crib, Moses basket, pram etc.

row to last 2 tr, skip next tr, 1 tr in top of beginning ch 3 of previous row. (16 treble clusters and 2 edge sts).

Rows 2 and 3 form pattern. Continue working in pattern for remainder of piece, working in stripes as follows:
Rows 4-5: 2 rows with col 1.
Row 6: 1 row with col 2.
Rows 7-8: 2 rows with col 1.
Rows 9-11: 3 rows with col 3.
Rows 12-13: 2 rows with col 1.
Row 14: 1 row with col 2.
Rows 15-19: 5 rows with col 1.
Row 20: 1 row with col 3.
Rows 21-22: 2 rows with col 1.
Rows 23-25: 3 rows with col 2.
Rows 26-27: 2 rows with col 1.
Row 28: 1 row with col 3.
Rows 29-33: 5 rows with col 1.
Row 34: 1 row with col 2.
Rows 35-36: 2 rows with col 1.
Rows 37-39: 3 rows with col 3.
Rows 40-41: 2 rows with col 1.
Row 42: 1 row with col 2.
Rows 43-44: 2 rows with col 1.
Fasten off.

Back and hood

Using col 1 and with RS facing, rotate work and fasten on at the marker to begin working along bottom of piece (this will be the fold line along the bottom of the bag). Continue working in pattern throughout in stripes as follows:
Rows 1-5: 5 rows with col 1.
Row 6: 1 row with col 2.
Rows 7-8: 2 rows with col 1.
Rows 9-11: 3 rows with col 3.
Rows 12-13: 2 rows with col 1.
Row 14: 1 row with col 2.
Rows 15-19: 5 rows with col 1.
Row 20: 1 row with col 3.
Rows 21-22: 2 rows with col 1.
Rows 23-25: 3 rows with col 2.
Rows 26-27: 2 rows with col 1.
Row 28: 1 row with col 3.
Rows 29-33: 5 rows with col 1.
Row 34: 1 row with col 2.
Rows 35-36: 2 rows with col 1.
Rows 37-39: 3 rows with col 3.
Rows 40-41: 2 rows with col 1.
Row 42: 1 row with col 2.
Rows 43-47: 5 rows with col 1.
Rows 48: 1 row with col 2. Place marker at each end of this row.
Rows 49-50: 2 rows with col 1.

Rows 51-53: 3 rows with col 3.
Rows 54-55: 2 rows with col 1.
Row 56: 1 row with col 2.
Rows 57-61: 5 rows with col 1.
Row 62: 1 row with col 3.
Rows 63-64: 2 rows with col 1.
Rows 65-67: 3 rows with col 2.
Rows 68-69: 2 rows with col 1.
Row 70: 1 row with col 3.
Rows 71-74: 4 rows with col 1.
Do not fasten off.

Form and seam hood

Fold the top edge of the work in half with RS facing together, join together along top edge with dc to form hood.
Fasten off.
Sew in all ends to WS of work.

Edging

With RS facing and using col 1, fasten on at the marker on the fold line. Begin working in rounds as follows:
Rnd 1: Ch 1, (placing marker or safety pin in first st) work 2 dc in each row edge of tr down left side edge, across hood, up

along edge to corner, 3 dc in the corner st, 1 dc in each st along front top edge, 3 dc in the corner st, 2 dc in each row of tr up right side edge, and ss to first (marked) dc.
Remove marker.

Rnds 2-5: Ch 1, 1 dc same place (replacing marker or safety pin in first st), 1 dc in each dc around edge, working 3 dc in each corner, join with ss in first (marked) dc.
Remove marker.

With RS facing, and front positioned over back ensuring edge of front lines up with markers placed at each end of Row 48 of back, place 5 markers evenly along the two front side edges to indicate placement of buttonholes.

Rnd 6 (Buttonholes): Ch 1, 1 dc in same place (placing marker or safety pin in first st), 1 dc in each dc to 1 st before first marker, (3ch, skip 3 dc, 1 dc in each dc to 1 st before next marker) 4 times, 3ch, skip 3 dc, 1 dc in each dc to top corner of front, 3 dc in the corner st, 1 dc in each dc along front top edge, 3 dc in the corner st, (1 dc in each dc to 1 st before next marker, 3ch, skip 3 dc) 5 times, 1 dc in each dc to end, join with a ss in first (marked) dc. Remove all markers.

Rnd 7: Ch 1, 1 dc in same place (replacing marker or safety pin in first st), 1 dc in each dc to first 3 ch-sp, (3 dc in 3 ch-sp, 1 dc in each dc to next 3 ch-sp) 4 times, 3 dc in next 3ch-sp, 1 dc in each dc to top corner of front, 3 dc in the corner st, 1 dc in each dc along front top edge, 3 dc in the corner st, (1 dc in each dc to next 3 ch-sp, 3 dc in ch-sp) 5 times, 1 dc in each dc to end, join with a ss in first (marked) dc.
Remove marker.

Rnds 8-10: Ch 1, 1 dc in same place (placing marker or safety pin in first st), 1 dc in each dc along side edge of back, across hood, along second side edge of back to top corner of front, 3 dc in the corner st, 1 dc in each dc along front top edge, 3 dc in the corner st, 1 dc in each dc along side edge of front, join with a ss into first (marked) dc.
Remove marker

Reverse dc edging

Change to col 2.

Next Rnd: Ch 1, 1 rdc in each dc around edge, working 3 rev dc in each of the 2 corners, join with a ss to first rdc.
Fasten off.

Finishing

Sew in all remaining ends and spray block. Sew buttons on back edging to correspond with buttonholes.

DONNA JONES
Donna designs, edits and teaches yarn crafts. She believes creative expression is essential for our wellbeing and aims to instil this in others. Follow her on Instagram
@djonesdesigns
www.donnajonesdesigns.co.uk

Crochet glossary

Asterisk*
A symbol used to mark a point in a pattern row, usually at the beginning of a set of repeated instructions.

Back loop (bl) only
A method of crocheting in which you work into only the back loop of a stitch instead of both loops.

Back post (bp) stitches
Textured stitches worked from the back around the post of the stitch below.

Ball band
The paper wrapper around a ball of yarn that contains information such as fibre content, amount/length of yarn, weight, colour and dye lot.

Block
A finishing technique that uses moisture to set stitches and shape pieces to their final measurements.

Blocking wire
A long, straight wire used to hold the edges of crochet pieces straight during blocking, most often for lace.

Bobble
A crochet stitch that stands out from the fabric, formed from several incomplete tall stitches joined at the top and bottom.

Brackets [ ]
Symbols used to surround a set of grouped instructions, often used to indicate repeats.

Chain (ch)
A simple crochet stitch that often forms the foundation that other stitches are worked into.

Chain space (ch-sp)
A gap formed beneath one or more chain stitches, usually worked into instead of into the individual chain(s).

Chainless foundation
A stretchy foundation plus first row of stitches that are made in one step.

Chainless foundation stitches
These are stitches that have an extra chain at the bottom so they can be worked into without first crocheting a foundation chain.

Chart
A visual depiction of a crochet pattern that uses symbols to represent stitches.

BLOCK

Cluster
A combination stitch formed from several incomplete tall stitches joined together at the top.

Contrast colour (CC)
A yarn colour used as an accent to the project's main colour.

Crochet hook
The humble tool that is used to form all crochet stitches.

Crossed stitches
Two or more tall stitches that are crossed, one in front of the other, to create an X shape.

Decrease (dec)
This is a shaping technique in which you reduce the number of stitches in your work.

Double crochet
The most basic crochet stitch

FOUNDATION CHAIN

Double treble crochet (dtr)
A basic crochet stitch three times as tall as a double crochet stitch.

Drape
The way in which your crocheted fabric hangs; how stiff or flowing it feels.

Draw up a loop
To pull up a loop of yarn through a stitch or space after inserting your hook into that stitch or space.

Fan
A group of several tall stitches crocheted into the same base stitch and usually separated by chains to form a fan shape.

Fasten off
To lock the final stitch with the yarn end so the crocheted work cannot unravel.

Fasten on
This is when you draw up a loop of new yarn through a stitch in preparation to begin crocheting.

Foundation chain
A base chain into which most crochet is worked (unless worked in the round).

Foundation stitches, chainless
See chainless foundation stitches.

Fringe
A decorative edging made from strands of yarn knotted along the edge.

Frog
To unravel your crochet work by removing your hook and pulling the working yarn.

Front loop (fl) only
A method in which you work into only the front loop of a stitch instead of both the loops.

Front post (fp) stitches
Textured stitches worked from the front around the post of the stitch below.

Gauge (tension)
See tension.

Half treble crochet
A basic stitch that is halfway between the height of a double and treble crochet stitch.

Increase (inc)
A shaping technique in which you add extra stitches to your work.

Invisible finish
This describes a method of finishing a round or edging so that the join is not visible.

Knife grip
An overhand method of holding a crochet hook, similar to holding a knife.

Linked stitch
A variation of any standard tall stitch that links the stitch to its neighbour partway up the post, in order to eliminate the gaps between stitches and form a solid fabric.

Magic ring
This is a technique to begin working in the round without leaving a hole in the centre, achieved by crocheting over an adjustable loop.

Main colour (MC)
The predominant yarn colour of a project.

Mattress stitch
A stitch to sew a seam that forms an almost invisible join on the right side of the work and a ridged seam on the wrong side.

Motif
Refers to a crocheted shape usually worked in the round as a geometric shape and combined with other motifs into larger pieces.

Parentheses ( )
Symbols used in crochet patterns to surround a set of grouped instructions, often used to indicate repeats.

Pencil grip
An underhand method of holding a crochet hook, which is similar to holding a pencil.

Picot
A tiny loop of chain stitches that sits on top of a stitch and creates a small round or pointed shape.

Popcorn
A combination crochet stitch that stands out dramatically from the fabric, formed from several tall stitches pulled together by a chain stitch.

Post
The main vertical stem of a stitch.

Post stitch
A stitch formed by crocheting around the post of the stitch in the row or round below, so the stitch sits in front of (or behind) the surface of the fabric.

Puff stitch
A combination crochet stitch that results in a smooth, puffy shape created from several incomplete half treble crochet stitches that are joined at the top and also the bottom.

Repeat (rep)
To replicate a series of crochet instructions; one instance of the duplicated instructions.

Reverse double crochet
A variation of double crochet that is worked backwards (left to right) around the edge of a piece, resulting in a corded edging.

Right side (RS)
This is the side of the crocheted piece that's visible.

Rip back
To unravel your crochet work.

Round (rnd)
A line of stitches worked around a circular crocheted piece.

MOTIF

Row
A line of stitches worked across a flat crocheted piece.

Shell
A group of several tall stitches crocheted into the same base stitch, which spread out at the top to create a shell shape.

Skip (sk)
To pass over a stitch or stitches.

Slip knot
A knot that can be tightened by pulling one end of the yarn. This is used for attaching the yarn to the hook in order to begin crocheting.

Slip stitch (ss)
A stitch that has no height, which is primarily used to join rounds and stitches to move the hook and yarn into a new position.

Space (sp)
A gap formed between or beneath stitches, often seen in lace patterns.

Spike stich
A stitch worked around existing stitches to extend down to one or more rows below, creating a long vertical spike.

Stitch(es) (st(s))
A group of one or more loops of yarn pulled through each other in a specific order until only one loop remains on the crochet hook.

Stitch diagram
A map of a crochet or stitch pattern, where each stitch is represented by a different symbol.

Stitch marker
A small tool that you can slide into a crochet stitch or between stitches to mark a position.

Swatch
A crocheted sample of a stitch pattern large enough to measure the tension (gauge) and test the pattern with a specific hook and yarn.

Tail
A short length of unworked yarn left at the start or end of a piece.

Tension (gauge)
A measure of how many stitches and rows fit into a certain length of crocheted fabric – usually 10 centimetres (4 inches) – that indicates the size of each stitch.

Together (tog)
A shaping technique in which you work two or more stitches into one to reduce the number of stitches.

Treble cluster (tr-cl)
A cluster of treble stitches, made into the same stitch or chain space and joined together.

Treble crochet (tr)
A basic stitch that is twice as tall as a double crochet.

Turning chain (t-ch)
A chain made at the start of a row to bring your hook and yarn up to the height of the next row.

YARN ROUND HOOK

V
The two loops at the top of each stitch that form a sideways V shape; standard crochet stitches are worked into both these loops.

V stitch
A group of two tall stitches crocheted into the same base stitch and then separated by one or more chains, forming a V shape.

Weave in
This is a tidying method that is used to secure and hide the yarn tails by stitching them through some of your crocheted stitches.

Whip stitch
A simple stitch to sew a seam by inserting the needle through the edge of both crocheted pieces at once to form each stitch.

Working in the round
Crocheting in a circle instead of back and forward in straight rows.

Working loop
The single loop that remains on your hook after completing a crochet stitch.

Wrong side (WS)
The side of a crocheted piece that will be hidden; the inside or back.

Yardage
A length of yarn, usually expressed as an estimate of the amount of yarn required for a project.

Yarn needle
A wide, blunt-tipped needle with an eye large enough for the yarn to pass through that's used for stitching crocheted pieces together and weaving in ends.

Yarn round hook (yrh)
To pass the yarn over the hook so the yarn is caught in the throat of the hook.

Yarn tail
See tail.

Yarn weight
The thickness of the yarn (not the weight of a ball or yarn).

TOP TIP
Use a yarn needle instead of a hook to weave the ends back through a project once complete. They will be more secure and less likely to unravel.

WORKING IN THE ROUND